WHAT'S YOUR STRESS STYLE?

Do you enjoy pulling the strings? Are you afraid someone else will control you?

Or do you crave approval? Are you sensitive to criticism and afraid to speak your mind?

Are you looking for the spotlight at the risk of your marriage?

Whatever your style, here's the doctor's prescription: preventive medicine to keep yourself in check and to cope with the people who drive you . . .

BONKERS

DR. KEVIN LEMAN is an internationally known psychologist and the best-selling author of *The Birth Order Book, Making Children Mind Without Losing Yours, The Pleasers,* and *Parenthood Without Hassles—Well, Almost.*

Dell Books by Dr. Kevin Leman

*Making Children Mind Without
Losing Yours*
The Birth Order Book
The Pleasers
Bonkers

BONKERS

Why Women Get Stressed Out
and What They Can Do
About It

Dr. Kevin Leman

A DELL BOOK

Published by
Dell Publishing
a division of
Bantam Doubleday Dell Publishing Group, Inc.
666 Fifth Avenue
New York, New York 10103

Scripture quotations from *The Living Bible* are copyright © 1971 by
Tyndale House Publishers, Wheaton, Illinois. Used by permission.
Scripture quotation from the HOLY BIBLE: NEW INTERNATIONAL
VERSION is Copyright © 1973, 1978 by the International Bible Society.
Used by permission of Zondervan Bible Publishers.

Material by Kay Kuzma excerpted from *Prime-Time Parenting*.
Copyright © 1980 Kay Kuzma. Reprinted with the permission of
Rawson Associates.

Copyright © 1987 by Dr. Kevin Leman

For information address: Fleming H. Revell Company, Old
Tappan, New Jersey.

The trademark Dell ® is registered in the U.S. Patent and
Trademark Office.

ISBN: 0-440-20339-2

Reprinted by arrangement with Fleming H. Revell Company

Printed in the United States of America

Published simultaneously in Canada

May 1989

10 9 8 7 6 5 4 3 2 1

OPM

To
my wife,
Bucky,
the love of my life,
whom I went bonkers over
twenty-two years ago . . .
I'm still bonkers for you!

Thank you to Frank and Patty Anderson, Martha Baker, and Faith Carter for their helpful assistance.

A special thank you to Paul Simpson for his valuable contributions in the research of *Bonkers*.

Contents

BONKERS

1

Why Is a Male Doctor Writing About Women and Stress?

"And what does he know about cramps and stretch marks?"

Wait, don't say it—I know you're probably thinking it. What does this male psychologist know about women and stress anyway? What makes him an authority on something he has no way of experiencing himself? When was the last time he tried to change a diaper, mop up spilled grape juice, and answer the telephone, all while getting his ribs kicked in by the new arrival due next month? And what does he know about cramps and stretch marks?

Before you banish me to the bookshelf, please hear me out. I admit I have a lot of gall venturing where even angels probably would never tread—but nonetheless, I have at least three reasons—I hope qualifications—for writing this book.

I've Talked to Hundreds of Stressed-Out Moms

In thirteen years of private psychological practice, hundreds of stressed-out women have come to my office with complaints that all boil down to one question:

"How can I keep from going bonkers?"

In most cases these women could be described as not only *stressed out* but also *draped out*—with young children. A common sight coming through my office doorway is a young mother with a baby in one arm, dragging her left leg behind her as she tries to find a chair. Does she have a neurological disorder in her leg? Not exactly—a two-year-old is attached to it!

In addition to learning about women's stress problems firsthand in daily counseling sessions in my office, I have traveled the country for the past ten years speaking to and talking with thousands of women who are "right on the edge." Many are stressed out far enough to want to walk out—just up and leave husband and children to find some peace and relaxation.

I recently read an article in *Woman's Day* that described the kind of mom I see all the time in my office or in church or school auditoriums where I speak. At age thirty-seven, with a two-year-old and a six-month-old clamoring for her attention, she wound up screaming in the shower for almost an hour, "I can't do it anymore. I can't meet all these needs. What about me?"[1]

It seems that in these final decades of the twentieth century, women have been liberated to join the work force, but someone forgot to tell their husbands *they* were also liberated to help get dinner on. My files show a marked increase in women wanting to leave their husbands and families—something that was rare just a few years ago.

So, what does all my talking with overstressed women accomplish? In hundreds of cases I have seen firsthand how women can learn to minimize stress and make it a useful tool by getting positive control of their lives.

3

My major purpose for writing this book is to share some basic practical ideas that will help you do the same.

That's one reason I think I can talk about stress and women, but I have others. . . .

I've Had a First-Class Teacher on Stress and Motherhood

That teacher, of course, is my lovely wife, Sande, who has been giving me training in understanding stress in women for at least twenty-two years. For nineteen of those years we've been married, bringing up Holly, Krissy, and Kevey. But she began even earlier than that. During the three years we dated before saying "I do," Sande taught me a great deal about the tremendous differences between men and women.

While advocates of the feminist cause have accomplished much that I applaud, one big mistake made by some of their more radical spokespersons is the claim that there are no real differences between men and women. They have equated *equality* with *sameness*. If there is anything I want to communicate in this book, it is that men and women are different, and *viva la difference!* In fact, I guarantee that when a husband becomes truly aware of the genetic, physical, and emotional differences between his wife and himself, he will be a better husband!

One obvious difference between men and women centers around sexuality. I see men constantly ignoring this difference, usually out of ignorance. I sympathize with a man who is baffled by his wife's lack of enthusiasm for sex when *he* wants it, because I was very naive myself during the first years of our marriage.

I thought the greatest thing we could share together was *copulating.* Sande taught me that the greatest thing we could share together was *communicating.* She taught me that a woman likes to be held and loved but not pawed and used. And she taught me that sex is a beautiful experience to share together as a natural result of communicating and loving each other. Sex is not to be simply the gratification of a natural urge.

Another part of my home training has taken place in Sande's absence, when I have had to walk in her homemaker shoes for as long as a day at a time. I remember one of those training sessions quite well. Sande left early in the morning and was gone all day, finally walking in at ten minutes to five. My first words were, "You're home! How many days have you been gone?"

"Days? I left at nine o'clock this morning."

I said, "You are kidding."

Sande walked into the family room and surveyed the chaos consisting of toys, tricycles, and other sundry objects scattered about the room. Sande is one of these "neat" women who like the home all shipshape. Her eyes narrowed as she turned to ask, *"What* happened?"

At that moment I knew the feeling of uselessness and hopelessness that many women face daily, if not hourly. I said, "I'm not sure. I straightened it up three times but I don't know . . . I mean, some kid was zooming through here on a tricycle a while ago . . . I don't even know who the kid was . . . and the twins from next door were over and, well, you understand. . . ."

Sande smiled as we tried to put the family room back into a condition fit for a family. She could have said something like, "Now you know what *I* go through all the time," but she didn't. She let me learn from my own experience, and that day I learned quite a bit.

Why Is a Male Doctor Writing About Women?

I felt the frustration wives feel when husbands and children don't pick up after themselves. You could call it the "banana peel syndrome." Somebody drops a banana peel somewhere near the middle of the kitchen floor. Hubby and the kids make several trips to the refrigerator or sink, but no one sees the banana peel and picks it up. Or, if they do see it, they step *over* it! Who has to spot the banana peel and pick it up? We all know who. No wonder so many mothers feel as if they are slaves or second-class citizens whose primary role in life is to clean up after the family.

Whenever I can, I urge the husband to try walking in his wife's shoes and learn firsthand what she is up against. My counseling and speaking, plus my happy though hectic life with Sande and our three children, ages fourteen, twelve, and nine, has sensitized me to the point where I believe I can intentionally think like a woman when it is necessary. I find this an invaluable tool in private practice, when it is important to "get behind the eyes of my women clients," to see life as they see it. As one mom told me:

> There are days when between driving the children to and from school,

taking my husband's shirts to the laundry ("light starch only, dear"), doing the grocery shopping, decorating the school cafeteria for the school fair, and picking up the house, I'm lucky to find time to go "potty."

This woman's perceptive comment only underscores a personal theory I've had for a long time: Men are unidimensional while women are multidimensional. We men do one or two things well and hold pity parties because we're "under so much pressure." I don't discount the pressure men face. I know a little about that, too. But I still believe that in comparison to men, women are multidimensional—able to wear many different hats and fill many different roles at once. I really can't prove my theory and I know some of my professional colleagues would explain it away by saying women *appear* more multidimensional simply because of the way our society is structured. But I'm not so sure.

I have thought a lot about how a woman's life changes when she marries and has children. Just compare her routine with her husband's. He still has lunch with colleagues and friends, plays golf, and attends Rotary. She

must adjust to diapers, dishes, and ne⅃
ing able to relax for more than forty-five
onds at a time.

Just observe the typical mother balancing a
precious ten-month-old, eighteen-pound object on her hip while she cálmly goes about
cooking breakfast, packing lunches, and talking on the phone. Ask a man to do all that at
once and you would have the lunches and the
ten-month-old all over the floor! After inter-
acting with hundreds of women who battle
the pressures and stress of family life day in
and day out, I am left with one firm convic-
tion: Men like to see themselves as wheels,
but women are truly the hub of the American
home!

Going Bonkers Is Not Inevitable

I hope by now you are becoming a little
more convinced that I know something about
stress and how women can learn to cope with
it. But you might still be thinking, *He talks
about women being stressed-out—but does he
really know how that feels?* I believe I do. In
fact, I *know* I do.

For my own personal story of too much

stress, I have to take you back to Friday, March 29, 1985. But we'll save that for later. First I want to share with you what I've learned about stress and how it takes its toll on busy moms and working women (who are often one and the same). Most important, we'll talk about how to prevent stress or at least keep it at a controllable level. We will look at six major areas of stress for many women that came to light in a recent survey I conducted. Those areas were, in order of importance:

CHILDREN Having them, caring for them, disciplining them, training them.

TIME Being overscheduled, dashing through life, living the typical hectic lifestyle that everybody thinks should be the norm today.

HUSBANDS Enough said.

MONEY Usually the lack of same, learning to manage it, learning to do without.

HOUSEWORK As one wife put it, "Housework we will always have with us."

> CAREER Over 56 percent of wives with children under eighteen are now in the work force.

My informal survey won't make the psychological journals, but it has helped confirm something I see in my counseling office: Today's women are under tremendous pressure to measure up in too many areas. In short, they are going bonkers in huge numbers!

The good news is that they don't have to. Going bonkers is not inevitable. Any woman can learn to reduce her stress level by practicing the commonsense advice in this book. I don't have esoteric or technical secrets to share, only simple principles that work—*if you use them.*

That last phrase is the key. This book can't help you unless you choose to let it do so. Today women are allowing society (their families, their peer group, the media, and other forces) to tell them what to do and be. But you don't have to put up with that stress-filled kind of existence.

Instead of feeling you are only one more crisis away from going bonkers, you can call your own shots. You can be the woman, wife, and mom you—and those around you—will be comfortable with. Those who love you will love you even more as you learn to handle your own stress and help them handle theirs as well. Believe me, there is a choice and the choice is *yours*. No one can make the decision for you.

What I have to offer isn't magic. When you get through reading this book, life will be as hectic and pressure-filled as ever. But the difference will be that you will have a much better idea of how to handle it. Believe me: *Bonkers is a preventable disease!*

2

Which Way Out of the Swamp of Life?

"Now that I have it all, I'd like to give some of it back."

"What happened, Dr. Leman? When we got married I thought my prince had come and we would ride off on his white charger to happiness ever after. Now it seems my prince has turned into a frog and I'm stuck with him in the Swamp of Life—with three more little frogs all croaking for attention. I have constant headaches, a nervous stomach, and I'm developing a twitchy left eye. What can I do?"

Almost every week I hear various versions

of the above refrain. It seems that Mom has had enough. She calls me, makes an appointment, and comes in to tell her story, which often has the same plot: She married young with bright-eyed expectations. Now she's trapped in an empty marriage that is full of disillusionment, three kids, and more stress than she can handle.

Her white knight from the long-ago wedding day is badly tarnished. It seems that in thirteen years, old Harry . . .

> . . . has washed the dishes twice.
> . . . has attended a PTA meeting once.
> . . . has never met the children's pediatrician.
> . . . hasn't spoken to his mother-in-law in two and one-half years.
> . . . went bowling on their last wedding anniversary (by himself).

Of course, there are some women who tell me they wish they could be so lucky as to have one as true-blue as Harry, who at least finds his way home by six o'clock every night. They describe their particular "prince" in grimmer terms, such as "workaholic," "alcoholic," or "womanizer." These wives are often in the early stages of going bonkers and are considering divorce as a last-ditch effort to salvage their sanity.

In Marriage, Stress Is Part of the Territory

From where I sit, the institution of marriage isn't simply under attack, it is in mortal danger. Today, between 50 and 60 percent of the couples who walk the flower-strewn aisle to exchange vows are condemned by statistics to march a rocky path to the divorce court— usually in seven years or less. Some so-called (or self-appointed) sociological gurus have loudly advocated that we allow the institution of marriage to become a quaint anachronism. In their opinion, long-term monogamy just doesn't work. To all this I say, "bullcrumble." The institution of marriage is just as healthy as ever: it's the people who enter it who need help, and one of their major symptoms is stress.

Granted, the typical married couple doesn't start out intending to fail. Wives, especially, expect their fair share of candlelight dinners, flowers, romance, attentiveness, and eventually bright, obedient, beautiful kids who get straight *A*'s. In short, they expect happiness, success, and married bliss.

It seems that someone forgot to tell them about the pressure.

Now, the young men and women getting married today aren't stupid—far from it. In fact, they are a sophisticated lot. They understand when parents, friends, pastors, or counselors tell them marriage will present plenty of problems and predicaments. But it's my strong suspicion that, while they hear this advice, they don't really *listen.* "We can handle it," they tell themselves. "With us things will be *different* because we are *really* in love."

What they fail to understand is that every marital love nest is a pressure cooker in disguise. After the wedding bells come the bills, the babies, and backed-up bathrooms.

Perhaps the most subtle pressure of all comes from the clock. As the wedding anniversaries tick away, time becomes more and more precious, more and more scarce. As I talk to wives who wind up in my office, it occurs to me that *it's a miracle they have had time to become disillusioned.* They have been too busy filling all the roles that marriage has thrust upon them.

I can recall one couple who came in to-

gether for counseling. The husband proceeded to put down his wife for not being
"up" on international affairs. She let him have
it right in front of me by saying, "How can I
be up on international affairs? I can barely
keep up with the notes the kids bring home
from school. I don't have time to read the
paper or even watch the news on television!"

Another wife I counseled decided to attend
the local university full time to study journalism. She finally had to switch her major, however, because she had one big problem: She
couldn't keep up with current events—a major prerequisite for journalism studies. It
seems that besides carrying a full load of
courses, she was expected to get home in
plenty of time to cook dinner and later clean
up, wash clothes, clean the house, keep the
yard looking good, and mother five children.
(The way she described it, four of the children
she had borne herself—the other one she had
married.)

The Swamp of Life Is Not Just Full of Alligators

The popular perception of the Swamp of
Life is that it is hip-deep in alligators. I believe

it's more accurate to say the Swamp is neck-deep in stress. Is there a way out? I believe there is, but getting out of the Swamp is not as easy as getting in. There is a little more to it than simply wading straight ahead.

If you have ever spent any time in a real swamp, you know how easy it is to get lost and wander in circles—literally forever. You need a compass, a map, or a guide to get out of any swamp—preferably all three. To get out of the mental and emotional Swamp of Life you must understand the stuff you are wading around in. What is stress? Does stress come from pressure or does pressure come from stress?

Because I'm not interested in chicken-egg arguments, I'll offer my point of view as a psychologist who specializes in helping moms, dads, and children. Stress comes from pressure—the tensions, emergencies, and the everyday minutia of life. In short, life is a pressure cooker and whether you remain serene or become stressed-out depends on how you handle that pressure.

Which Way Out of the Swamp of Life?

Stress Is Destroying Cathy

A mom we will call Cathy is a dramatic example of a lot of women I see who handle pressure the wrong way. At age thirty-four, she is a homemaker with four children ages three to twelve. Her husband, Bob, is an accountant who is busy climbing the corporate ladder of success with a large company.

Not surprisingly, Bob sees parenting as "mostly women's work" and he depends on Cathy to do almost all the disciplining of the children. While he won't admit it, Bob wants Cathy to mother him, too, and he depends on her for the answers to heavy questions such as, "Where's my shirt? Where are my shoes? I have to be at the office in thirty minutes!" And then he tears off to work long, hard hours to "provide for the family."

And how is Cathy handling this scenario? Actually, she isn't handling it at all—she is simply maintaining a precarious status quo that is driving her more bonkers by the day. By her own admission, she lost control years ago. Her kids back-talk and make fun of her. She overreacts with screaming, yelling, and striking them too often and too hard. Naturally this makes her feel guilty, and so the vicious cycle continues.

"I'm not the mother I should be," she tells me in my office. "Why can't I have more patience?"

The answer to that desperate inquiry is easy for me to see, but not so easy for Cathy, who is a composite picture of many women I counsel. She has allowed herself to be put under tremendous pressure by her undisciplined children and an uninvolved husband who thinks that working long and hard at the office justifies his coming home to demand that the children be quiet while he relaxes from his "impossible day with the boss." He spends little or no time with the kids and, following his two-hour after-dinner nap, he expects Cathy to be ready to "fool around a little" at bedtime.

Cathy, of course, is not only exhausted but also full of anger and resentment because Bob is never there to pitch in around the house the way he could. She feels like a combination maid and geisha girl. Under these conditions, sex with Bob sounds as thrilling as cleaning the garage.

But Cathy keeps wading through her own Swamp of stress, rationalizing the whole mess by buying into the lie her husband tells her (and himself): "Hey, why do you think I'm going out there and busting my tail? I'm doing it for you and the kids!"

Sad to say, Cathy believes, just as Bob does, that his job, success, stature, and rising salary are the most important things in life. Everyone in Cathy's family suffers from their crazy schedule, but the one who suffers most is Cathy herself. She is a classic example of the kind of mom who comes to my office at the end of her tether. Mothers like Cathy often have physical symptoms in addition to emotional problems such as guilt, anger, and frustration. Being over-stressed shows up in heart palpitations, cold sweats, colitis, indigestion, and headaches—particularly migraines, which Cathy battles periodically.

The Cathys of this world try to cope by seeing a doctor. They spend hundreds of millions of dollars a year on prescription and nonprescription drugs. Additional millions are spent on alcohol—all in an attempt to escape from the pressure cooker called the American Way of Life.

When someone like Cathy comes to me, she hopes I will be able to sprinkle some magic "psychological dust" that will help her cope with her indifferent husband and impossible children. Of course, I have no magic dust. But I do have some practical advice. What Cathy needs is a basic understanding of what stress is, and then she needs to learn some basic skills to cope with her pressures and identify the areas in her life that result in too much stress.

Without getting technical, I'd like to give you a short course in stress to show you just how life's pressures turn into something we can't quite see but we certainly feel as we wade through the Swamp of Life.

Why Stress Can Be Such a Deadly Foe

For our short course in stress, we will look at the ideas of two men:

1. Dr. Hans Selye, the grand old man of stress researchers who "discovered" stress back in the 1930s. Selye has written many papers and technical books on stress. His three nontechnical books for general readership are *Stress Without Distress*,[1] *From Dream to Discovery*,[2] and *The Stress of Life*.[3]

2. Dr. Richard Ecker, founder and director

of Life Management Institute and author of
Staying Well,[4] and *The Stress Myth*.[5]

I first became acquainted with the writings
of Dr. Selye years ago in my undergraduate
training at the University of Arizona. Selye, of
course, didn't discover stress. He is more correctly identified as one of the first to identify
stress as a cause of disease in the human body.
One of his basic contributions to our understanding of stress was what he called the General Adaptation Syndrome when he published various books and papers in the 1950s.
The General Adaptation Syndrome, or G.A.S.,
includes three stages: the Alarm stage, the
Resistance stage, and the Exhaustion stage.[6]

Here's how the General Adaptation Syndrome works: Our bodies have been wonder-
fully designed by our Creator to respond to
peril and danger in very definite ways. When
we perceive any threat through our bodily
senses of sight, sound, smell, or touch, our
nerves send a message to the pituitary gland
in the brain, which manufactures what is
called the adrenocorticotrophic hormone—
more simply known as ACTH.

The ACTH hormone travels through the
bloodstream to the adrenal glands, which are
attached to the kidneys. It is here that the

body manufactures the well-known substance we call adrenaline, which most of us associate with getting "pumped up" for athletic contests or for any other event that requires strong physical effort.

The job of the adrenal glands is to increase our heart rate, raise our blood pressure, increase our breathing, and release sugars and fats into the bloodstream. All of this gets our bodies ready for the next stage, which is Resistance, or what Selye called "fight or flight." We fight stress physically, psychologically—any way we can. If we are successful, the threat to our well-being disappears and our body relaxes with the help of the parasympathetic nervous system. Our breathing rate and blood pressure return to normal. Tenseness in our muscles slowly dissipates. The pupils of our eyes, which had become enlarged, return to their regular size.

Usually as we deal with various stresses in life, we hope to experience only the first two stages of the General Adaptation Syndrome Selye talks about: Alarm and Resistance. For example, suppose you are zooming along in traffic, heading for work. You are momentarily distracted as you fiddle with the radio dial. You look up and see that traffic has stopped for a red light. You are about to rear-end the car in front of you! Now you are in the Alarm stage and the adrenaline is pumping through your veins. You hit the brakes (you are in the Resistance stage) and skid to the stop only inches from the bumper of the car in front of you.

As you wait for the light to turn green, you move through the final stages of Resistance as your body returns to normal. Your heart was in your throat and now it seems to be settling down. Your legs feel wobbly—like rubber. You can barely press the gas pedal as the light turns green and you pull away to continue driving to work. By the time you get to work, you are probably "back to normal." You have handled the stress of a near collision and everything is okay again.

But suppose you go into work and immediately face a crisis with your boss. He is angry because you didn't get a report due yesterday to him on time. Once again you go into the Alarm and Resistance stages. Perhaps you handle the first encounter with your boss with no problem, but suppose he comes back in an hour or so with another complaint, and then another. Suppose this goes on for several days, even weeks. Now the stress starts to pile up. If things get bad enough, you will wind up in what Selye referred to as the Exhaustion stage, and here is where you can collapse under pressure.

During the Exhaustion stage, there is an enormous amount of wear and tear on the organs of the body. It is in the Exhaustion stage that we develop colitis, high blood pressure, ulcers, and even heart attacks. Many of the wives and mothers who come to my office are in some form of the Exhaustion stage.

As Richard Ecker points out in his helpful book *The Stress Myth*, "Unquestionably, stress is the most significant negative health influence at work in the American society today. . . ."[7] He believes our society is devastated by stress because we like to believe that stress is inevitable, that we are victims of a complex world that is out of our control. Ecker maintains that all this is a myth and that we spend too much time in what he calls stress *intervention* (learning techniques such as biofeedback, meditation, and hypnosis) and not enough time in stress *prevention*—learning techniques to get stress under control and not letting pressure develop into too much stress—or as Selye put it, *dis-stress*.

Ironically, many of the women who come

to see me have caused their own state of distress—that is, too much stress. Like Cathy, described earlier, they have bought into the lie of needing to have it all right now. Why is it that a society as richly blessed as ours has more stress than any society in history? One basic reason is that we don't want to wait.

When I was a kid growing up in western New York, I seldom saw a Mercedes or a Cadillac, and when I did the driver almost always had graying hair. Now, in the course of a typical day, it's not uncommon to see several Mercedes or other expensive automobiles tooling through town with one or more preschoolers riding in their car seats, and their Yuppie-age mom at the wheel. Can moms and dads this young afford a Mercedes? Possibly some can, but a lot of them cannot, and that is why Dad has to work long hours at the office and why mom might have to take a job as well.

It all adds up to the kind of stress that can't be taken care of by going through a simple process of Alarm and Resistance—fight or flight—and getting it over with. The kind of stress we see permeating society today is the ongoing, ever-present, exhausting kind that wears down wives, husbands, and children—entire families.

My counseling load makes a strong case for the charge that today's family is in a state of crisis due to prolonged stress. It is no exaggeration to say that our families are in the Exhaustion stage. I find more and more young adults who are afraid to marry. They look at the older generation—my generation—and see that we haven't done very well maintaining the honorable institution of marriage. Over half of all marriages end in divorce and the number of households headed by single mothers is at a new high. The average marriage lasts a whopping seven years. (Chances are, your G.E. refrigerator has a life span twice as long as the average marriage.)

Another startling statistic claims that only 14 percent of all families are what could be called "traditional." By traditional I mean a mother and a father in a first marriage, children growing up in a home where Dad is the principal breadwinner and Mom stays at home to take care of them.

Another statistic that bothers me is that the average American home owner stays in one place for only seven years. Recently I was interviewed by a reporter for a large newspaper. He was doing a feature on the changing population shift in our country from the northeastern states to the Sun Belt. He asked me where I thought people should live and because I'm from Tucson, Arizona, I'm sure he expected me to tout the warm, dry climate of the Southwest.

He looked surprised when I told him that married couples should live as close as possible to at least one set of grandparents. He thought I had misunderstood his question, but I assured him I understood perfectly.

"What I'm trying to tell you," I said, "is that today's families have really missed the boat. They've become little nuclear units that wind up far away from the wonderful support of the extended family. My generation had the pleasure and advantage of growing up surrounded by aunts, uncles, and cousins. That can be a real source of strength, and that's why we take our children back to western New York every summer to visit my sister and her family. We've also been lucky enough to have both sets of grandparents with us here in Tucson."

My reporter friend went away shaking his head. Perhaps he was in one of those nuclear family units himself. If so, his kids might only have been able to see Grandma and Grandpa every other year at Christmas. Perhaps they knew nothing about aunts and uncles, who all lived in other parts of the country. They may have had to face the constant problem of just starting to make some friendships that could add stability to their lives, and then coming home to learn that Mom and Dad were moving on to bigger and better things in another city hundreds or even thousands of miles away.

Does all this put the American family under an undue amount of stress? You answer the question.

Meanwhile, Which Way Out of the Swamp?

I always get a bit antsy with simply hashing over a problem. I like to look for solutions. The rest of this book will offer a lot of ideas for analyzing your stress and coping with it, but for general openers on what to do about stress, I'd like to share Hans Selye's "secret recipe" for dealing with the pressures of life.

In his excellent book entitled *Stress/Unstress,* Keith Sehnert tells of being present when Selye met with a group of doctors, nurses, and other scientists one day in 1977.[8] Selye was asked to summarize a paper on

stress that he had presented earlier that day.
He came up with three ingredients for his
"secret recipe":

1. *Know your own limits.* Test yourself to
   see if you are a racehorse or a turtle.
   Then develop a life-style that fits you
   and no one else. (We'll be looking at
   that whole area a lot more in chapter
   3.)
2. *Choose goals that are right for you
   and your life.* Be sure they are *your*
   goals and not something that is forced
   on you by parents, teachers, or other
   people. Whatever you do, be sure it's
   what you choose to do. Selye told the
   group that when people try to live out
   choices others make for them, it only
   causes suffering.
3. *Look out for yourself by looking out
   for others and earning their goodwill.*
   Selye calls this "altruistic egotism." By
   helping others you help yourself as
   you make your deposit in the other
   person's "bank of good will."

In his book *Stress Without Distress,* Selye
calls this third step "earning your neighbor's
love."[9] We have no closer neighbors than

members of our own families. Ironically, I talk to many mothers today who are getting a bit weary of trying to practice Selye's principle, which Jesus stated in the form of the Golden Rule. One of the unfortunate messages women are getting out of the feminist movement is that they should look out for themselves, seek their own fulfillment, and so on.

Of course, I don't blame these women. For centuries men have made a fine art of putting themselves first. We have failed to see that we are much better off when we really get to know our wives and do our best to please them. Again and again I hear women in my office telling me they would live anywhere—even in a tent—if their husbands would just put them first. At the very bottom line, women aren't interested in financial success as much as they are in being cherished, prized, loved, and respected by their husbands.

So now we see more and more women going out into the work force, not only to pay the bills but also to find fulfillment. More and more women are arriving in my office agitated, angry, upset, and depressed—what we term in the vernacular, "stressed-out to the max." More and more women are developing heart conditions, high blood pressure, and cancer. More and more women are finding out that "having it all" is not what it was cracked up to be. They tell me they would like to give some of it back.

Keep Selye's three suggestions in mind as we continue on with our look at how to keep from going bonkers, which is just another way of saying "how to keep from being over-stressed." Now that we've laid down some simple definitions for stress, it will help to take one more "short course" in personal psychology. How "stressable" are you? It depends on your personality—your basic lifestyle. Everyone is susceptible to pressure and stress. You may, however, be leading with your chin, and I'll explain more about that in the next chapter.

3

How Stress Prone Are You?

"Are you a controller, pleaser, martyr, or . . . ?"

In his excellent little book *The Stress Myth*, Richard Ecker maintains that it is wrong to say your job, marriage, or other parts of your life are "stress filled." Your life, says Ecker, includes *sources* of tension, pressure, and change which you can *perceive* in various ways. It is your *perception* of something that turns it into a *stressor* (threat) to your well-being. As soon as a stressor exists in your mind, you have stress.[1]

As we saw in chapter 2, there are times

when stress is most appropriate. When you are about to rear-end a car, it is perfectly proper to perceive this as a real threat and hit the brakes! But other stress can be excessive and inappropriate. When the boss gets on your case every morning, you can perceive it as a problem or you can realize the boss has arthritis and is never very human until after a three-martini lunch.

Unfortunately, in your case, the boss's crabby attitude really bothers you and you are just about ready to quit. Why is it that Marge, whose desk is next to yours, just brushes off his tirades and even seems to curry his favor? The answer lies in perception. You perceive the boss one way; Marge perceives him another way. Your perception causes you great stress. Marge sails through without a qualm.

Why the difference? Simply because we are all different—particularly in regard to perceptions. Our perceptions are based on what we experience, and no one experiences anything exactly the way someone else does. That's why certain sources of tension, pressure, and change can bring out different responses. It all depends on how we interpret what is happening to us.

Let's explore this a bit further. Exactly why do we perceive and experience things so differently? Many schools of psychology believe the answer lies in our past—particularly childhood. How we grow up is critical to how we perceive things as adults. My particular training is called "Adlerian," named after Alfred Adler, a pioneer in Individual Psychology. Adler believed that during childhood every person learns what he called a style of life or "lifestyle." Adler wasn't talking about developing a taste for designer clothes or fast sports cars; by "style of life" he meant the way people function psychologically to reach their goals. Adler always claimed that if he knew a person's goals, he could pretty well predict how that person would act and live.

As we pursue our goals, we develop a certain perception of how we fit into the world, and we filter everything through that perception. We also develop what Adler called "lifelines," but he did not mean the creases in the palm of your hand. Because Adler's definition can get very technical, we'll keep things simple by interpreting lifelines as the "lines of talk" we feed ourselves and learn to believe as accurate pictures of who we really are.

I suppose you could say there are as many

life-styles as there are people on the face of the earth, but this wouldn't help us nail down some broad categories into which we might fit. And I do see some broad categories every week in my office. The basic life-styles I see include the controller, the pleaser, the attention getter, and the martyr. All of these people feed themselves certain "lines" of talk.

For example, the controller, naturally enough, tells herself, "I only count when I am in control." The pleaser says, "I only count when I make others happy." The attention getter feels, "I only count when I am noticed." And the martyr believes, "I only count when I suffer."

As we try to understand stress and its effect on our lives, it helps to take a look at life-styles and see how one style invites more stress than another.

Controllers Are Powerful People

I run across two main kinds of controllers in my practice. Some strive to control everything and everyone because they are on a power trip. They really do enjoy pulling all the strings.

The other kind of controllers, however, want power for a totally different reason: fear. They become controllers for defensive purposes, because they fear that someone else will take control of them! Following are some basic characteristics of controllers. Remember, a controller doesn't have to have all of these traits. Normally he or she is a blend of some of them.

Controllers keep it all in and then explode. They can hide their feelings for a time but when they get to their boiling point—*boom!* The explosion is usually a violent one that takes it toll on those around them, particularly their loved ones. This kind of controller has a real temper and is quite capable of throwing tantrums.

Controllers have a tremendous need to be right. They are often found in precise and structured occupations such as engineering, executive secretarial work, accounting, architecture, or computer programming. Controllers love to argue and they seldom lose.

Controllers keep people at arm's length. They can go into a meeting and glad-hand everyone in the place, yet no one ever gets to know these people. They are skillful at avoiding intimacy. I often counsel couples that include one spouse who is a controller who refuses to be open and intimate. The other spouse pries, coaxes, pleads, and pokes with pitchfork in hand, so to speak, but the mate simply retreats into a shell and won't come out.

Controllers tend to fear death. What is death but an ultimate loss of control in life? No wonder death scares a controller. Sometimes these people also fear losing their minds. If they are dreamers, they tend to dream about being chased and falling. They always wake up just before they hit.

Controllers are often perfectionists. They have deep-seated fears of inadequacy because they feel as if they always have to measure up but don't quite make it. These perfectionist types always have to clear what I call the "high-jump bar of life." And even when they clear the bar they tell themselves they could have done a little better.

Controllers tend to be critical people who in almost all cases have critical fathers. Fathers are a key in producing critical daughters.

Controllers are insecure, shy, or temperamental. They can manipulate others through tears and temper tantrums.

As I mentioned before, controllers operate

on the power principle. Some use their power in a wide-open, dominant style with lots of shouting, table pounding, and fireworks in general. Others are the quiet types who, on the surface, seem pleasant and gentle and loving. Their families know differently. By now it should be obvious that controllers can cause others a lot of stress, but that doesn't mean they are immune from stress themselves. In fact, controllers usually experience more stress than any other life-style. When a person tries to control everyone and everything, it's easy to see problems or pressures as threats. The threats become stressors, and stress results.

I remember in particular Nancy, who came to see me in a state of exhaustion. I soon learned that she controlled her entire family, and even her friends, through guilt. Nancy manipulated everyone subtly, by doing a lot of "worrying." When her daughter asked, "Mom, can I go with Suzy to the beach?" Nancy would reply, "Well, I guess so, but you know how I worry when you're around water."

Nancy also managed to worry about her husband losing his job, her children's future, the weather, political unrest in South America, and anything else she could latch on to. I had a hard time making her see that her worrying was a subtle source of controlling others around her, but once she got the message, her stress level went down significantly.

Stress Prevention Tips for Controllers

If you are a controller, the stress may be getting to you. When I deal with moms who admit they are controllers, I suggest at least three steps:

1. *Lighten up.* This is so obvious, you probably wonder why I would charge anyone for that kind of counsel. It's amazing, however, how many controlling wives and mothers believe they must have everything and everyone under their thumb or they can't function. No wonder they are under stress. It is obvious that no one can control everyone and everything. So I make it a point to ask these controlling women to tell me where they think they can let go in regard to their children or their husbands.

"Perhaps you could let little Annie make some decisions about what clothes she wants to wear."

41

"Perhaps George has better taste in restaurants [or movies or vacation spots, etc., etc.] than you give him credit for. Why not let him choose next time?"

2. *Realize that being less controlling doesn't mean things are out of control.* Controlling moms are often very fearful that if they do lighten up on the children, all will be lost. They remind me, "I thought you were big on Reality Discipline, Dr. Leman. Are you telling me to become permissive?" As we shall see in chapter 7, Reality Discipline of children does not mean holding them in an iron grip. It does mean giving them choices. It's amazing how you reduce your own pressure (and the resulting stress) when you make other people responsible for their own decisions instead of always having to make decisions for them.

3. *Remember that to love those in your family you must be able to let them go.* Some moms who need to be in constant control really bristle at that one. What do I mean by saying they don't love their husbands and children? They are simply trying to do *what is best for everyone!* To paraphrase a famous line from a well-known movie, "Love never has to say, 'I only wanted to do what was best for

you.'" Love frees; it does not grasp, hold
down, or control.

Tips for Those Who Live With a Controller

For women who are controllees—that is,
married to controllers—I offer the following
suggestions:

1. *Refuse to play your husband's controlling games.* Remember that the minute you
enter into the game he wants to play, your
stress will begin. I often advise working wives
to not fall for the old line that goes like this:
"Sure you can work—just have dinner on by
six." I suggest gentle confrontation and a mature discussion of how both of you can share
the chores at home. Granted, sometimes this
works and sometimes it doesn't but it is always worth a try.

I remember counseling one woman who
had an extremely critical husband. He ham-
mered her about financial matters in particular and kept her on a tight budget. No matter
how frugal she was, he would criticize her
when she ran out of money, which almost always happened because he simply didn't give
her enough. Finally, she got tired of it. Nicely

but firmly, she handed all the bills and the checkbook back to her husband. He tussled with the finances for three months and wound up increasing the budget *significantly* before pleading with his wife to take back the bookkeeping chores!

2. *Realize that your controlling spouse probably isn't going to change a great deal.* This may sound like giving in, but it is a basic key to avoiding stress.

3. *Accept your spouse's controlling habits without perceiving them as direct attacks on you or your character.* When he is crabby, dominating, or sullen, you don't have to perceive it as a direct reflection on you. Remember the rule we learned earlier: Any source of pressure, tension, or criticism doesn't become a stressor and turn into stress *unless you perceive it as a threat.*

A lot of wives I counsel are becoming stressed out at home because their husbands, children, or someone else threaten them in some way. When I help them realize that what's happening is really no threat but simply a fact of life, they make huge strides toward being more relaxed.

Grace, age thirty-one, was an example of a wife who felt threatened by a woman who worked for her husband. Grace was happily married to Ralph, an extremely successful businessman, but she found herself becoming jealous of Linda, Ralph's executive assistant.

Linda was superassertive, confident—a real dynamo. Ralph talked about Linda constantly and was obviously very dependent upon her at work. This bothered Grace to no end because she felt Linda was more important to her husband than she was. Every time Ralph talked about Linda, Grace became tense and upset.

When Grace called to make an appointment to see me, she said she was feeling very stressful because of three small children. But as she shared her parenting problems, she kept mentioning Ralph and "this assistant he has at work." By our third session together, Grace poured out her story and then I asked, "When Ralph talks about Linda, does he give you the impression he thinks she is a better person than you are, or does he simply seem grateful for Linda's help?"

"Well, I'm not sure. All I know is that she sounds pushy and obnoxious."

"Wait a minute—you said she was confident and capable. How do we get pushy and obnoxious out of that? A lot of your stress is probably coming from your perception of Linda, which could be entirely wrong. Why don't you talk to Ralph and simply tell him how you feel?"

Grace was dubious, but she finally leveled with Ralph. Much to her surprise, he didn't laugh at her or get angry. All he said was, "I guess I do talk about Linda quite a bit, but only because she is a good worker. She's a good assistant, but I'd hate to have a perfectionist like that for a wife."

Ralph's comment helped Grace realize Linda was no threat to her at all. Grace finally saw that she was doing herself a real disservice by comparing herself to her husband's executive assistant when there was really no basis for comparison at all. The entire incident helped Grace relax and feel more secure around Ralph. Her stress problems with her children diminished as well.

Pleasers Need to Be Liked

The direct opposite of a controller is a pleaser (yes, you guessed it—I often find pleasers married to controllers).

Pleasers want the oceans of life to be

smooth. They need approval from everyone —particularly other family members.

Pleasers are extremely sensitive to criticism, and will work very hard to make things just right for all concerned.

Pleasers are afraid to speak up about their true feelings, because the truth might result in rejection. That's why pleasers are the kind of people who go along with others. They are skilled at reading social signals and knowing how to give in to keep everyone happy.

Pleasers often live behind a phony mask. While they are shaking their heads in agreement, they disagree strongly in their hearts and they hate themselves for their own cowardice.

Pleasers usually have low self-esteem. They don't feel their two cents is worth even that much. That's why they try to build their self-image by covering all the bases and doing everything for everyone.

Perfectionists are often pleasers. As I mentioned before, controllers can be perfectionists, too, but in the pleaser, perfectionism shows itself in a different way.

Two of the most stress-filled pleasers I have ever met were Bernadette and her husband, Gene, who were both extremely active in a fundamentalist church where Gene was an elder and Bernadette was Sunday-school superintendent, women's Bible-study leader, and a deaconess.

I call Bernadette and Gene "pedestal people" because they thought they always had to be the perfect example. The family had all kinds of problems. Gene and Bernadette weren't all that happy together, and they were also struggling with the parenting of their four children.

As I talked with them, I could see that their stress level was extremely high. Bernadette in particular felt constant pressure to be the perfect elder's wife, as well as the perfect Christian. This family was so trapped in the pleaser lifestyle that having some ordinary fun on vacation caused them tremendous guilt and apprehension. Gene and Bernadette came to see me following their vacation and confessed that the family had gone to several movies, attended an amusement park, and had even eaten in a restaurant where liquor was served. They were sure God was displeased with them. It made me think the God they worship must have the biggest slingshot on record!

"If anyone in our church hears about this, we'll be kicked out," Gene told me.

As pedestal people, Gene and Bernadette felt they had to constantly measure up, measure up, measure up. People are watching—always watching—and you must be perfect. You must do this and do that to please everyone and keep the oceans of life perfectly smooth.

Even though their children were fairly normal youngsters, being parents caused Gene and Bernadette tremendous tension. What would be considered normal problems and scraps in most families were disasters in theirs. If one of the children got sent to the principal's office, for example, it meant being grounded for a month, plus other penalties. When their teenage daughter started slipping away to be with friends whom Gene and Bernadette considered "wild," the tension was fierce. And when she lied to cover herself, her parents were beside themselves.

While Gene showed a great deal of stress, it was Bernadette who really concerned me. She was so full of stress it appeared to me she was one short step from going bonkers. I zeroed in on their perfectionism and strove to help them see that they were imperfect people—no matter how dedicated to God they believed they were. In fact, what really got them to change was that I convinced Gene, the pleasing head elder of his church, that if he really wanted to do God's work on this earth he had to learn to share his imperfections with others.

"Did you come to terms with God out of victory or failure?" I asked Gene. "I believe the Bible says something about God not being very happy with the proud, but always being willing to help the humble. If you become humble enough to share your faults and problems with other church members, they'll be more willing to share their lives with you."

As for Bernadette, she was tired of being up on a pedestal. I asked her, "Just how comfortable do you think the women of the church are when they have to keep you up there on that pedestal?" Bernadette looked at me hard. "I see what you mean," was all she had to say.

For the next several months, Gene and Bernadette worked hard at opening up and sharing their imperfect selves with other church members. Interestingly enough, people didn't reject them and turn away. In fact, they made several new friends and were even able to help their pastor come down off *his* pedestal somewhat.

All of this helped Gene and Bernadette start communicating and begin pulling their marriage together. Bernadette relaxed when she stopped trying to be involved in everything and jump through every hoop in order to please everyone, especially Gene, from whom she had felt tremendous pressure to be the perfect wife.

As Gene and Bernadette came down off their pedestals, they were able to relax in their parenting roles. While they remained strict, they were more willing to listen to their children and try to be more understanding. The entire family made such good progress that they ended counseling after just a few months with the stress level well under control.

At their final session Bernadette told me, "It's great to be down off the pedestal. I'll never go back up there again!"

Stress Prevention Tips for Pleasers

Whenever I talk to moms who are pleasers —and I talk to a lot of them—I give them the following suggestions:

1. *Learn to say no.* Have the courage to stand up to your family and not do everything for them. Moms are often suckers for cleaning up after everyone. At our office we have a sign in the little coffee break corner that says, "Your mother doesn't work here. Please clean up after yourself."

2. *Stop apologizing for your every thought and word.* What you have to say is important. I realize you don't gain high self-esteem with a snap of the fingers, but the first steps toward a better self-image include having the courage to speak your mind. Who knows? The controllers in your life might do a double take and decide to show you a little more respect.

3. *Realize that by not trying to please everyone all the time you are not being unloving or a "bad" person.* On the contrary, letting others do for themselves is a great way to show them love. How else will they ever learn to be responsible and to act on their own? This is particularly true when rearing children. There is no better way to set your child up for

failure than to always "do it for him" to be sure he is happy and pleased with you.

Attention Getters Want the Spotlight

Attention getters have a lifeline that reads, "I only count when I'm noticed." Attention-getting characteristics include the following:

Attention getters are often last born, the babies of the family. Babies are often written off by older siblings and they develop an "I'll show you I can do it" attitude. Last borns often show off to gain the spotlight and the respect and admiration of others in the family.

Attention getters can also be first born in the family. The first borns usually gain attention by doing everything right, being cooperative, getting good grades, and so forth. This is a constructive approach to gaining attention. The destructive approach is to be a pain in the neck or to act like a know-it-all. The point is, the attention getter gets what he is after by manipulating the people around him to always remind, coax, nag, or congratulate him.

Attention getters are carrot seekers. They do

good things and then ask, "Where's my carrot?" What they want is reward and praise.
Carrot-seeking attention getters do a lot of
things for others, but they have hidden agen-
das. They keep telling themselves, "I only
count when I'm noticed, so people had better
notice me or else!"

*Attention getters are first or second cousins
to controllers,* and I meet a lot of moms who
qualify for the label to one degree or another.
In its milder forms, attention getting can be
irritating to others in the family, who get tired
of loud talking, boisterous laughter, and
someone who always has to be in the limelight
and is always wondering "why people don't
do as much for me as I do for them."

At the more serious levels, attention getting can ruin marriages. I recall a thirty-eight-
year-old businessman who craved attention
so badly that he wound up in affairs with several women in his employ because his quiet,
homebody wife simply didn't pay enough attention to him and give him the strokes he
was after.

How to Cope With Attention-Getting Behavior

If you are married to an attention getter, try the following:

1. *Don't play the attention getter's games,* particularly if the means employed to gain attention are negative. For example, if your husband's attention getting makes you feel uncomfortable, tell him how you feel—and why.

2. *Directly confront the attention getter, calmly and lovingly.* When the attention getter makes a fool of himself, say, "Look, I get uncomfortable when you do things to call attention to yourself. I like it when you act like yourself—not someone else."

3. *Don't ever let an attention getter use you as the brunt of his jokes.* Tell him, "No one likes being used—especially your wife."

4. *Give the attention getter positive strokes when he refrains from his "look at me" behavior.* Be careful, however, not to pat him on the head or patronize him. Instead, say something like this: "I really appreciated how you acted with the Smiths at dinner. You were clever and classy and I was proud to be your wife."

If you realize you are an attention getter, here are some positive steps you can take:

1. *Be continually aware that to need attention is a mark of immaturity.* For example, if you need all the attention in your marriage relationship, you are acting selfishly at the expense of your family.

2. *Stop seeking carrots.* See how many nice things you can do for people without expecting recognition or payback. You will find the "emotional carrots" won't be so important.

3. *Deliberately try to put other people into the limelight,* ahead of yourself. Some simple ways to do this include letting your husband do some of the talking when you are out with friends; letting your quiet neighbor have you over for coffee instead of always insisting that she come to your place.

Martyrs Think They Only Deserve to Lose

The martyr's favorite line is, "I only count when I lose, suffer, or don't get very much."

Martyrs often have a poor self-image. They seek out people who will reinforce that negative self-image—particularly the people they marry.

Martyrs are good at finding people who will walk on them, use them, and abuse them. Alcoholics are often married to martyrs. A martyr is an excellent mate for an alcoholic because he or she makes excuse after excuse and coddles the alcoholic, all the while thinking that this is the way to show "real love."

A poor relationship with the opposite-sex parent often helps to develop a martyr personality. I talk to a lot of women who are martyrs and discover that they did not have a good relationship with their fathers. Gerilynn, thirty-four, married, and mother of three, kept telling me during counseling, "I'm no good, I'm nothing, I'm kept in the dark. He does whatever he wants to do with the finances—all he wants me for is sex and a housekeeper."

It turned out that Gerilynn's husband controlled everything. They had only one car and he took it to work every day, even though he could easily have used public transportation.

Ironically, Gerilynn's husband was a fairly good provider, but a very frugal man with both his money and his conversation. He was the classic "man of few words" and seldom communicated with his wife or children.

I asked Gerilynn to describe her father and

here's what she told me: "He was very strict, a man of few words, a good provider, and he could control you with just a look. He was very frugal, from the old school, and he had a violent temper that I saw only twice and that was enough."

Then I asked Gerilynn to describe her mom and, of course, we got the precise opposite: "Very loving, very patient. She'd give you the clothes off her back. She was strictly a homemaker and she cared for other people's children from time to time to make a few extra dollars."

The picture for Gerilynn was quite clear, and it had been painted years before when she was a child. She was the classic martyr and was now facing desertion by her husband, who was getting involved with another woman. At least this had made her angry enough to come see me and try to get some help.

"I let him be head of the house," she bristled, "but where does it get me? What does it all get me?"

I explained to Gerilynn that allowing her husband to control her, as he had been doing, was getting her nothing but being walked on. By submitting so completely to her husband,

she had turned into a dishrag, and no man
likes to pursue a dishrag. That's why he had
found someone else.

I talk to many women who have been
taught to be "submissive wives." The trouble
is that they swallow this line so completely,
they become doormats and dishrags. They
often start out as pleasers and wind up martyrs because their husbands take advantage of
them. At best, they live unhappy, frustrated
lives; at worst, they are often victims of abuse
and mistreatment.

*Martyrs have a knack for latching on to
losers.* They marry alcoholics, wife beaters,
and drug addicts. It is simply uncanny. If
there is a loser out there to be found, the
martyr can sniff him out faster than a springer
spaniel can flush a pheasant.

At age thirty-three, Susan was a classic martyr. Divorced three times, she was contem-
plating a fourth marriage and came to see me
on the advice from some good friends who
strongly suspected that this one wasn't made
in heaven, either.

Susan had known Tony for just three and
one-half months, but she was already "madly
in love." The more she told me about Tony,
the less encouraging it sounded. Tony had a

very bad family background. Deserted by his mother at age nine, he was raised by his father for two years and at eleven went to live with his paternal grandmother in another city. I tried to explain to Susan that when a son does not have a stable relationship with his mother, usually he is not a very good bet for marriage.

Susan didn't care about the odds. She wanted Tony—more accurately, she *needed* him. One of the incredible needs in this woman's life was to always have a man. As I talked with her, I discovered that over a period of twenty-five years—since age eight—she had always had a boyfriend or a husband.

A lie a lot of women tell themselves is, "I simply *must* have a man." Something I always try to communicate to women clients is that a man is an option, not a necessity. As my colleague and friend Sonya Friedman puts it in the title of her book, *Men Are Just Desserts.*

With all the signals turning up negative, I did my best to convince Susan not to jump into marriage. If she felt that strongly about Tony, why not continue dating him but plan not to marry for at least two years.

Of course, it took a lot less than two years for the real Tony to surface. In four months

Susan broke off the engagement because she got a taste of how hostile and angry toward women Tony could really be. And where did Tony get that hostility? We only have to go back to that day his mother deserted him.

When you are a potential princess looking for your prince, time is your best ally. One piece of advice I often give women is "Stay out of bed."

Surveys of male sexual habits reveal that men don't usually want a woman to go to bed on the first date. They wait until the second. The first date is simply to get acquainted, to say, "Hi, how are you doing?" But when a man comes back for a second date, he usually expects a roll in the hay, and a lot of women are suckers enough to believe that if he doesn't get it he's gone forever.

My obvious questions to these women are these: "If all he wants is a roll in the hay and he stops seeing you if he doesn't get it, what have you lost? If he has to have sex on the second date, how serious is he about building a truly intimate relationship?"

Women with martyr life-styles have a very hard time with such questions. This is especially true if they are women like Susan who have been divorced two or three times already. I am totally convinced, however, that when a woman allows a man to become physically intimate without the commitment of marriage, she destroys the potential for building anything real or lasting.

It may be a difficult concept to sell, especially in these days of "enlightened morality" (*benighted* is more like it), but the psychological facts are there. Many men fear real intimacy. They also tend to work out their problems and hang-ups sexually. If they feel poorly about themselves, they think the best way to prove otherwise is to "score" and to conquer. And they love to prey on women who believe they only count if they have a man and are willing to do anything to get one.

Stress-Prevention Tips for Martyrs

It's not too hard to see that martyrs are pleasers who have let life get out of control. Their husbands and children have them so stressed out they are in a perpetual state of exhaustion. They have, for all practical purposes, given up. To help the martyrs out of the Swamp of Life, I tell them the following:

1. *Loving is not letting your children or*

husband walk on you. This is particularly needful advice for the wives of alcoholics. I believe that most of the television advertising for alcoholic treatment centers is designed to reach the martyr wife and help her get the backbone to do something about her husband's problem. In almost every little "episode" in one of these ads, the wife has finally put her foot down and made the husband call a particular treatment center.

2. *Take some positive steps to build your self-esteem.* Quit telling yourself lies like, "I only count when I'm suffering and I don't deserve anything better than this anyway." You can go through life believing that garbage or you can change. This is why I try to help people find a good church where they can develop a real faith in God. Somebody said it this way: "God don't make no junk!" I'd like to add to that and say that God don't make no martyrs—at least not the kind who appear in my office.

3. *Realize you are your own worst enemy.* Martyrs like to think the world is out to get them, that others are doing all the dirty work to them. In truth, the martyr does the dirty work to herself. I can recall Gail, a thirty-nine-year-old homemaker, who came to me with a

self-diagnosis of "chronic depression." Gail was married to a very unemotional, mechanical computer programmer who had drained Gail's life of any zest and enthusiasm whatsoever. Living with Ralph made watching the grass grow an absolutely heart-stopping event by comparison.

I startled Gail when I asked where her depression came from. Why it came from Ralph, of course, she answered. I told her it sounded as if she thought she had caught a chronic case of depression from her husband. In truth, she *chose* to be depressed. Depression doesn't come from outside, it comes from inside. When her husband was insensitive, forgetful of her birthday, or bought her something tacky and void of taste, what did she do? She told me, "Well, I get depressed. I think he makes me depressed."

"No," I told her. "You *choose* to become depressed. You feel bad because your husband isn't what he is supposed to be, so in essence what you do is go out of your way to show him how miserable he has made you feel."

I urged Gail to try something new: to shock her husband by refusing to reinforce his boorish behavior.

"Try telling him how you feel about colors like orange and purple together, about western art, cubic zircons, or gold-plated necklaces—or whatever. First of all, you have to decide that you have some feelings and you have a right to express those feelings in a positive way. Maybe, Gail, you can become a teacher to Ralph and help him learn there is more to life than what he sees right now."

Gail tried it and, while Ralph didn't change all that much, Gail did. Instead of perceiving Ralph's behavior as something that threatened her and depressed her, she started looking at things differently. Her depression lifted and she was able to live a happier life.

Remember Where Stress Comes From

There are many other life-styles we could discuss. Variations of the controlling life-style include people who tell themselves, "I only count when I win," or "I only count when I succeed." There is an awful lot of talk today about winning as society operates for the most part on a win-lose basis. Always having to win or succeed is a perfect way to put yourself under enough stress to kill you.

Variations of the pleaser life-style are many,

and one of the most prevalent I see when counseling church members is the idea that "I only count when I serve God." I counsel many people who are so busy serving the Lord they are candidates for a stress breakdown. Ironically enough, their faith, something that is supposed to give them peace and fulfillment, is draining and exhausting them. The Lord isn't their Shepherd. He's foreman on their chain gang.

What kind of life-style do you have? What kind of lifeline do you hand yourself every day? You may fit some of the categories we discussed, or you may have your own particular version or emphasis. Whatever your life-style may be, it will cause you stress. Sometimes the stress can be good and help you achieve what you need to get done. But in many cases the stress can be destructive and toxic. The way to prevent that kind of stress is to change your perceptions.

Easier said than done, you're probably thinking, and you're right. But you can do it, a little here and a little there. In fact, let me say you *must* do it because stress will come at you —and does—from every direction. We'll look at some of the major sources of stress in your life in chapter 4.

4

The Six Biggest Stressors in Mom's Life

"On certain days, being a mother is the pits."

"What causes stress in your life?" is a question that brings a barrage of answers from women of all ages. I surveyed women and came up with six sources of potential stress among married women, with and without children, plus a large number of single mothers. Before I list these six potential "enemies," let's see how many of them you can find working on Teri, a thirty-three-year-old mother of three, who had almost every one of the big six driving her bonkers.

When Teri came to see me she had been married for eleven years. Besides teaching preschool part-time, she mothered three children of her own, ages eight, six, and four. That would have been enough to keep most women occupied, but Teri was just getting warmed up. She also ran a Brownie troop, taught Sunday school, coached Bobby Sox softball, and collected for the United Way!

Teri's husband, Joe, was general sales manager for a small manufacturing company and his job required that he travel quite a bit, leaving Teri to "hold the fort" most of the time.

Teri's life-style was in the pleaser category. Her main mission in life was to have everyone like her, particularly her kids and her husband. A pretty blond, Teri appeared in my office looking tired and haggard, like many women I see. She told me she woke up tired, that she felt as if she were "losing control." She reported shortness of breath, sweaty palms, and a few times she had felt "as if her heart were in her mouth."

Teri openly admitted that she no longer liked herself. "I'm screaming at the kids, I'm not a good mother. I'm not a good wife either —I resent Joe and the long hours he puts in on the job. I don't even like to come home from my preschool job at night. I resent having to clean up the kitchen and do laundry so the kids can have clean clothes for school."

Teri's self-esteem was at an all-time low. She was losing sight of what life was really all about and she wasn't sure if anything mattered anymore.

The Fast Lane Is No Place for Tricycles

Things weren't going exactly as Teri had planned when she and Joe got married. She had everything down pat back then. She would work for a while until Joe's career got off the ground, and then she would raise her family, just as her mother did back in Ohio.

But now Teri was caught traveling in the fast lane with only a tricycle for transportation. Here was a woman who started her mornings with her stomach in knots and who ended most of her days with headaches that would force her to lie down and remain perfectly still until the pain and nausea subsided enough to allow her to function.

She admitted that on many occasions she would find herself sleeping during the day when she wasn't at work. Or she would come home from work, sleep through dinner, and wake up in the early evening realizing she hadn't fed the children yet. This latter routine was especially attractive when her husband was out of town on business.

Somehow, though, she functioned flawlessly in her part-time job as a preschool teacher. She didn't have enough help to handle the fifteen four-year-olds in her care, but she smiled her way through. She was proud of her reputation as "one of the best teachers in the school."

Like many others in the same predicament, Teri had a hard time understanding why things were falling apart. After all, she and Joe were enjoying financial success and "freedom." They had a new five-bedroom home with a pool, two brand-new cars, and a housekeeper who cleaned two days a week. On the surface, it looked as if Teri and Joe had everything going for them. Why, then, was Teri ready to run?

The Six Biggest Stressors in Mom's Life

Teri Wanted to Leave It All Behind

Teri was one of the new breed I see more and more of in my office. She was severely disillusioned with marriage and her instincts were telling her to get out. Teri, like a lot of women today, wanted to run away and leave her husband and children—just leave it all behind her.

I asked Teri, "What are your husband's main priorities in life? Give them to me in one, two, three, four order, if you can."

Teri responded that those priorities were: (1) his job; (2) financial security; (3) his children; (4) his parents.

"And where do you fit in?" I wondered.

"Well, I guess I fit in there somewhere—probably fifth."

Teri obviously had many problems, but I could see that a major one was Joe. Her husband certainly wasn't showing the kind of leadership a man should give a marriage. Any time a wife isn't right at the top of her husband's priorities, that marriage is in trouble.

Doubly tragic about the whole situation was that, when Teri tried to send Joe a message about how she felt, it backfired. Whenever she brought up the need for them to get away together or just spend some time alone, Joe would annihilate her emotionally by reminding her that he was only out there, "doing everything I can for you and the children." And the worst part of it was, Teri believed him!

Teri was a textbook case of a woman who had fallen into today's classic trap: going for it all. She was telling herself that to be fulfilled she had to work outside the home, drive the nicest car, live in the nicest house, and be a loving wife and mother as well as an active church member and volunteer worker, all without a hitch. She was caught on an endless treadmill and stress was draining her into a state of total exhaustion. No wonder she wanted to run away.

I knew that running wouldn't accomplish a great deal, but before I tell you how I tried to help Teri out of her Swamp, let's see if you identified the several areas that had become sources of her stress.

Children Are Stressor Number One

As you probably guessed, the number-one stressor in a group of almost two hundred women I surveyed was children. Teri's big problem with her three kids was discipline. Because she was a pleaser, she tended to be permissive. Her part-time job meant that her own children had to spend a lot of time in the care of baby-sitters or, in the case of her four-year-old, at a private day-care center.

Her kids resented her working and let her know it, when she got home, with various forms of misbehavior. Like many working moms, Teri had a classic case of the "guilties" and this led her into being permissive. Instead of using a firm hand, Teri tried to placate her kids by being a "nice mom" and she let them get way with a lot more than they should have. The result was that, practically every night, the bedtime ritual ended with Teri screaming at all three kids, after she had been pushed beyond her limit.

Undoubtedly, Teri would have put her own kids right up there at the top of the stress list, as did most of the moms I contacted. If Teri's particular problem doesn't quite fit your situation, see if you can find yourself in the following random sample of remarks moms made to me:

A twenty-year-old mom with a nine-month-old has trouble at the end of the day, "when things don't go my way, when dinner burns, when my son screams and nothing will soothe him. . . ."

Most mothers are familiar with experiencing stress when little things go "Wah" in the night. A twenty-three-year-old mom with a six-month-old admitted being stressed by "the crying, fussing, screaming my baby does —not being able to sleep with night feedings, etc."

Of course, babies don't cry through the night forever. They grow up to be two-year-olds. When I read the following it was apparent that, for this twenty-nine-year-old mom, life with her two-year-old was a scream, but the wrong kind. "Being on the phone and child screaming right underneath me, being in a public place and child screaming, driving the car and child screaming," were the times that caused her stress.

Then there was the twenty-five-year-old mom with children two and one, and she was expecting a third! Not surprisingly, she had the strength to write only one word on her questionnaire? "Fatigue!"

When the kids get a little older, the sources of stress are different but no less intense. A thirty-two-year-old mom with children twelve and eight said she gets stressed, "when my kids don't use any common sense. When they don't mind at all." A thirty-six-year-old mom with kids ten and five felt stress by "having to act as a referee between my children."

Of course, as the children reach the teens, things get better, right? Not for a lot of moms I talk to. A thirty-eight-year-old mother was stressed by her fourteen-year-old's grade problems, plus his constant hassling of his nine-year-old brother.

One thirty-nine-year-old mother of two teenagers told it like it was at her house: "You've got to be kidding! The eighteen-year-old is late from dates and her ear is to the phone all the time. My fifteen-year-old has a chronic illness. I'm overextended timewise, and my husband procrastinates on household responsibilities."

The teenage years often bring stress in the form of worries about how the kids are doing academically and socially. One forty-three-year-old mom with two teenagers worried about her children's school performance plus their lack of friendships and their poor self-image.

A forty-seven-year-old mother with daughters twenty-one and nineteen and sons fifteen and twelve said, "I'm stressed by wondering if my daughters will find good husbands who have the same faith they do. One daughter has had thoughts of suicide since thirteen. The girls seem to live for the present rather than plan for the future."

And so the cycle repeats itself. Stress and children come together and there is no way to avoid it. There are some things you can do to lower the stress level, and I'll talk about that in chapters 7 and 8. Meanwhile, let's get back to Teri and the other pressures that were burning her out.

The Clock—and Stress—Run Hand in Hand

The number-two stressor in my survey of wives and mothers was lack of time. Obviously, Teri fit this bill perfectly. Her incredible schedule left her with little energy, and when something unexpected came up she was totally wiped out. What really threw her was having any of the children become ill, even for a day or so. There simply wasn't any time allotted for flu, colds, and so on.

At one session I was only half joking when I asked Teri if her children had to schedule stomachaches or skinned knees. Teri's time crunch was severe, but to one degree or another the very same problem surfaces everywhere. In my survey of moms, one of the chief stress complaints centered around the clock, the work load—the fatigue.

The phrase that popped up again and again was, "Too much scheduled." For a lot of women, however, it isn't a case of compulsively wanting to do too much; it's simply being forced to do too much because of all the responsibilities that come home to roost right on Mom's doorstep.

A twenty-seven-year-old pregnant mother summed up major causes of stress in her life as, "Trying to plan a meal without knowing when my husband will be home. Moving into a new home and still having lots of boxes to unpack. Having too many things planned for one day, and not being able to finish."

A twenty-six-year-old mother of a one-year-old child said, "I work part-time, so getting to work, getting a good baby-sitter, and still getting the house cleaned, meals made, time with my son, causes stress."

One mother of three children, ages three to eight, said poignantly, "It seems that *everything* and *everyone* is vying for my time!"

Another mom with kids thirteen and twelve exclaimed, "Too many battlefronts!"

The daily battle closes in on women. One thirty-two-year-old mother with children eight, five, and three described causes of stress in classic terms: "My three children, mealtimes, bathtimes, bedtimes, my oldest son's homework, my husband when he drinks —THE PHONE!"

In these quotes from overworked and overscheduled moms, you may have noticed a certain word popping up a great deal: *husbands.* In my survey of major stressors for moms, husbands finished number three, just a point or two behind pressures from the schedules and the clock.

Husbands Cause Stress in Many Ways

"Disagreements" seemed to be a key source of stress between wives and their husbands. Wives become stressed over disagreements about how to discipline the kids, disagreements about how to spend the money, and disagreements over coming home late, to name just a few. As one wife put it, "My husband is always late—he'll be late for his own funeral!"

These basic kinds of disagreements often turn the wife into a nag. Women know they shouldn't nag but they still feel thrust into the role. One woman felt a lot of stress from being "a nagger to get him to do simple things like washing, changing clothes, etc."

Many wives don't feel too much oneness with their husbands. One wife reported stress from the "physical and mental absence of my husband too often, mental absence of myself too much, lack of spiritual harmony with my husband, not enough prayer."

Another wife, twenty-one, with an eight-month-old child, reported a husband who "leaves important decisions up to me. No good communication between us. I don't even get ten or fifteen minutes away and free of the responsibility of the baby."

A thirty-six-year-old wife with a ten-year-old didn't mention her husband but did say there was a "lack of open, verbal communication, a prevailing attitude of uncaring" in her family.

A fifty-one-year-old woman with five grown children ranging from twenty-two to thirty-three years old experienced heavy stress because of her "husband's temper and general attitude toward me. Nothing I do is of any importance. Only what he does is important."

Feeling that they are the only ones who care is quite possibly the biggest stressor of them all for many women. One mother expressed it as "feeling that I am the only one who does anything around the house."

Teri, the subject of our case study, could relate to that one. We've already covered Joe's lack of involvement at home and his failure to put Teri high on his list of priorities. I'll say it again for emphasis:

> When a wife isn't high on her husband's list of priorities—and by "high" I mean right up there at the top—it is bound to become a source of stress for her.

When women get married, they expect to be loved, cherished, respected, and adored. When that doesn't happen, and hubby spends most of his time at work, the wife is threatened. When she is threatened she becomes stressed, and when the threat continues, the stress can wear her out.

Like many wives who are trying to hold

down jobs while raising families, Teri was overworked and overcommitted, but that wasn't the real cause of the nagging, pervasive fatigue that overwhelmed her. The real cause of her fatigue was the tremendous stress she felt because Joe simply wasn't interested in working with her and helping her.

When there is a basic lack of oneness with your husband, stress hits harder from all directions. I believe Teri was also feeling financial stress, even though she and Joe had more than enough money to buy what they thought was important.

"Wanting It All" Is the Root of Much Stress

The fourth major stressor, according to my survey, is money—financial problems. While Teri and Joe seemed to have this one solved—at least in the sense of having plenty of money to buy what they thought they wanted—I still think they had financial problems. For most of us, money problems center not in what we need but in what we want, and we usually want too much. Joe and Teri wanted it all, and no matter how much they made it was never quite enough.

"Too much month at the end of the money" was a frequent source of stress I found in my survey of wives and mothers. Raising kids is expensive, but even wives without children complain, as did one twenty-nine-year-old woman who felt stress "when the bills pile up and the paycheck isn't big enough."

Everything has a price, and stress is often part of the price tag. A fifty-one-year-old woman whose three children were long grown and gone reported her stress package came wrapped in a new daughter-in-law and a dog that had just dug up forty dollars worth of newly planted flowers!

It's hard to pin down why many families struggle with money. There might be a real problem or there could simply be a continuing struggle with living in a consumer society that tempts us to spend ourselves right into stress, more stress, and finally bankruptcy.

Whatever their reason for working, women come home from one job to find another one waiting. My survey revealed housework as the fifth most stressful pressure on women because so many of them have to hold down two jobs: one at the office and one in the kitchen and laundry room.

Stress Is Ironing Shirts After 8:00 P.M.

Significantly, housework was a major problem for Teri, even though she could afford to bring in someone to clean twice a week. There were still the meals to prepare when she came home from work, the kitchen to clean up, laundry to be done, clothes to be ironed for school the next day, and so on.

Teri got no help from Joe, who was out there every day to "do it for her and the kids," and then collapse in front of the TV every night. The result was that she tended to procrastinate. She had no organization or routine to attack the housework. In fact, the whole situation was attacking her and she was ready to surrender.

A lot of women I surveyed were not necessarily ready to surrender in their war with housework, but they certainly weren't winning, either. Out of all the women I talked to, only *one* said she enjoyed housework! For some women, other pressures leave them with little energy to combat the dirty dishes and heaps of laundry.

A thirty-two-year-old wife with no children admitted stress because, "First I get bogged down worrying about my job. Then I worry about paying the bills, even though it's my husband's responsibility to pay them. By the time I get home from work I'm so bogged down I don't feel like doing any housework."

Sometimes we think that housework becomes a problem when there is an overwhelming list of chores and responsibilities. But one mother, age thirty with three children from ages two to seven, found plenty of stress in simple things like, "spilled milk or overflowed toilets." What got to another mother with only one child, age ten, was "company coming, especially parents and in-laws."

Sometimes it's not the housework per se that becomes the stressor; it's the *timing*. A twenty-seven-year-old mother with a one-year-old and husband who worked a lot of overtime admitted that, "the five o'clock hour is very stressful, with my son miraculously knowing the time to be most demanding and crying and tugging at my legs while I make dinner. I am so tired I want to go to bed when my little boy does—at eight o'clock!"

How about women who don't work outside the home? For many stay-at-home moms there are stress problems in "just being a housewife." A twenty-seven-year-old mother with kids one and three said that for her stress was "seeing slender, perfect-looking mothers with spotless homes. Not having a 'real job.'" A thirty-year-old mother with a five-year-old and a newborn expressed her stress by adding, "When people around me forget that being a mommy is a valuable and hard job, too. People think you have to be a career woman."

What that last mom didn't realize is that being a mother and homemaker *is* a career, one that a lot of women have to neglect when they decide to go into the work force. One of the biggest lures dangled in front of women by the advocates of "having it all" is a "real career," the glamour and fast pace of the workaday world, having people doing your bidding and even obeying your orders, having your own credit card and "taking your husband to dinner . . ." just like the woman executive in the credit card ad on TV. But there is a price for all this and the price is high.

Don't Expect to Leave Home Without Stress

Sixth among the causes of stress, many women told me, was "the career." Teri loved her job teaching preschool—and she was good at it. She prided herself in handling those fifteen preschoolers with little or no help. She was so proud of the "professional skills" she used at preschool that she failed to see the terrible irony in the screaming sessions she had with her own kids at bath and bedtimes.

Teri isn't the only mother I've talked to who finds herself in a vise when trying to mix two careers. A twenty-three-year-old wife with no children finds plenty of stress in the "pressure at work—just driving down the freeway."

A twenty-nine-year-old single mother with a three-year-old and a six-month-old found stress in a "job with high dress and low wages." She wanted to educate herself to advance her career but was unable to do so due to working long hours "just to make ends meet."

A working wife complained of "deadlines at work, and customers who are extremely difficult to deal with."

A thirty-eight-year-old mother with a teenager and a twelve-year-old found her job stressful because, "I'm in a 'people business' and the constant relating and analyzing can create tension."

Because the working mom is an ever-increasing phenomenon (56 percent of all moms with children eighteen and under are working, according to latest statistics), we'll take a closer look at them in chapters 9 and 10.

So What's the Answer to All This Stress?

By now you've probably had enough examples of the "big six of stress." You've identified with several of them yourself and you'd like to know, "What can I do about all this?"

And what about Teri? What magic potion did Dr. Leman prescribe for this stressed-out, part-time career woman who had a pseudohusband and a false concept of what family life is all about? Actually, the story of Teri and Joe has a happy ending, because they did some basic things to prevent and eliminate a lot of the stress in their lives. In chapter 5 we'll finish their story as we start discovering the "secret" of keeping stress under control.

5

The Simple "Secret" to Reducing Stress

"Give me some pills or something —some kind of exercises to relax. . . ."

At the end of chapter 4 we left Teri, a thirty-three-year-old stressed-out mother of three, sitting in my office asking me, "Which way out of the Swamp called 'my life'?"

Teri had come to me because she knew she was trapped. She couldn't get much help from Joe, her tuned-out husband, who was busy climbing the corporate ladder to the stars down at the office. Joe just kept saying, "I'm doing all this for you and the kids!"

Teri's three kids were no help, either. They

were reacting like normal eight-, six-, and four-year-olds whose mom wasn't around often enough—whining, mouthy, not minding. All they knew was that Mom wound up screaming a lot—especially when they wouldn't go to bed.

The fifteen preschoolers Teri taught part-time might have felt bad if they had been told, "Teacher is not feeling well," but about all they could have done was send a big get-well card.

In short, none of the people in Teri's life could help her out of her Swamp. They *were* the Swamp—or were they?

Teri sat in my office staring at me, her big blue eyes dulled by fatigue: "Well?"

It was time for Dr. Leman to give his complicated diagnosis.

"We have a psychological term for your condition, Teri. It's called a mess."

"I already *know* I'm in a mess," she snapped. "Give me some pills or something—some kind of exercises to relax. . . ."

"Oh, we can do all that," I said, "but that only treats the symptoms. You need to get to the cause—the root of the problem—the reason you keep setting yourself up for failure."

Teri didn't like the word *failure*. After all,

she and Joe had three healthy kids, two new cars, and a lovely home. She handled fifteen preschoolers with ease. How could that be failure?

"Yes, and you are depressed, exhausted, and unhappy with your husband and children. Your stomach is in knots, your head is pounding like a tom-tom, and you're stressed to the breaking point. This is what we call *success?*"

"Well, when you put it that way, I suppose you are right."

"You suppose I am right? If I'm not right, why are you here talking to me? What you have to do is change some things—and the sooner the better. The good news is that most of the changes will be fairly simple—and some will even be fun."

Teri was all ears at the mention of "simple" and "fun." One of my first assignments for her was to think about this: "What is the most important thing in life?"

"I used to think it was my husband and children," she said, "but now I'm not so sure anymore. Joe is so busy working, all he seems to want from me is maid service and some sex when *he* isn't too tired. When I'm around the kids all they do is fight and hassle me. It seems that everyone wants a piece of my flesh and I have no time for myself."

"Then let's start right there by looking over that almighty schedule of yours and making sure you do one thing a week—just for yourself."

Teri Starts Out of Her Swamp

And so Teri made a start in getting out of her Swamp. Her "one thing for me" was taking an aerobics class, something she had always thought would be fun, but there had never been time. Now Teri *made* the time and enrolled in a YWCA aerobics program three nights a week. Strangely enough, she felt stronger and more full of energy than ever before.

The next thing we tackled was her role as co-breadwinner. Her part-time job took a big chunk out of her week. Those fifteen pre-schoolers were taking an enormous amount of her energy.

Teri loved her job, so it was not easy to get her to take an objective look. When she did, she admitted, "I'm beginning to realize I've been taking care of everyone else's kids and watching them grow up, but I've been missing out on my own."

It wasn't that Teri was a neglectful mom—not at all. She tried to cover the bases, rather ingeniously, in fact. For example, Tami, her eight-year-old daughter, was involved in a play at school, but of course Teri couldn't attend because curtain time was 1:00 P.M. and she was busy with her preschool class. Teri felt quite proud that she had asked another mother to videotape the play so she could view Tami's performance later on the VCR.

"Very commendable," I told Teri at our weekly session. "You have solved the problem of not being able to see your daughter perform, but you have not solved the problem of having an eight-year-old looking out in the audience and not seeing her mom there to applaud."

(Of course, it would have been quite proper to discuss how Dad might have been there, too—even sales managers have been known to take an afternoon off—but at this point we were working on Teri's Swamp. Joe's would come later.)

The Case of the Videotaped Performance led to Teri's next major decision. She was realizing that she couldn't change her husband, she couldn't change her kids, but she could change her schedule. At first Joe was shocked by Teri's decision to quit teaching preschool at the end of the term, only a few weeks away. At the same time, Teri sensed that he was quite pleased. Joe was getting more than a bit stressed himself and he could see that this "having it all" attitude was taking its toll on everyone—and especially on Teri's physical and emotional well-being.

"I Can Get Out—I AM Getting Out!"

So we were making some progress out of the Swamp, but there were occasional alligators to contend with. I spent several sessions with Teri helping her get through what I call "life-style withdrawal." She was a pleaser by nature and the idea of putting herself first was hard to swallow.

"You made some difficult choices," I explained, "and you should feel good about them. You are worth it. You deserve some 'down time' when you're not on the go every minute to make the schedule."

Teri struggled for a while, but slowly it all came together. Taking the aerobics class and not coping with fifteen preschoolers resulted in a more-relaxed and less-haggard Teri. She still had problems with her own kids, but now she was there to cope with them on a full-time basis.

Over the next few months Teri became much more comfortable with herself and with her kids. The Swamp wasn't as deep and she started feeling, "I can get out—I *am* getting out!"

The family missed her paycheck, of course, but not as much as Teri had feared. She could see why life had been happier for Joe and her the first couple of years of marriage, when they had struggled financially, but had had more time together.

Slowly we broke down the hard shell Teri had built around herself. Underneath we found a softer Teri who really wanted to become more involved in a positive way in the lives of her children and her husband.

Joe Joins Teri in Counseling

At this point I suggested that Joe join Teri in counseling. He hesitated at first, but then decided to come. (Perhaps his wife's example helped him see he could miss a few hours at the office after all!)

One of the first exercises I had both of them do was to list the three or four most important things in their lives. I told Teri it might be fun to put down what she would have said when she first came to see me, and them make a second list to see if anything had changed.

They both busied themselves with pencil and paper. About five minutes later I had them read their lists aloud to each other as I listened.

Joe's list didn't surprise me. It read: "First, family; second, job; third, financial security; fourth, recreation (jogging)."

Teri's two lists were revealing. When she had come for her first appointment, she believed her list would have read: "First, children; second, husband; third, job; fourth, church." Now she believed her list would read: "First, children; second, myself; third, church; fourth, husband."

Joe looked a bit surprised at his fourth-place showing on Teri's second list, which represented how she felt about him at the moment. Later, I talked to Joe alone, while Teri waited outside. I explained that Teri had him listed fourth because I had been working with her to make some time for herself.

"Is that really such a good idea?" he wanted to know. "I listed my family first and so should Teri."

"Well, Joe, actually that's your problem. You've been telling Teri you work long hours and come home dog tired because you're doing it for her and the kids, but that sounds a little hollow when you don't spend much, if any, time with the children and you never help Teri with the house and getting ready for the next day, when you both have to go out and do it all over again."

Joe stared at the rug. "I guess I don't get very involved. It's just that I'm so tired from putting in ten to fourteen hours on the dead run."

"I understand. I go home from this office the same way some nights. But I've learned from talking to a lot of clients that men and women use different love language. For many of us men, the way to say 'I love you' is to go out caveman style, so to speak, and 'bring home the bacon'! Then we tell ourselves—and our wives—the big lie that is built on faulty beliefs: 'I'm doing this for you and the kids!' "

"But I am!" Joe protested.

"Maybe you think you are, but the truth is that we men like to do our thing and build a career and let our wives take care of the rest of it. As I said, it's a caveman instinct and it's been around a long time."

"Building a career is important to me—is that wrong?"

"No, not wrong, but the question is, how important should it be? I think you need to come to grips with reality and admit that the most important thing in your life is your job—at least Teri thinks so. The first time she came to see me, I asked her what she thought your priorities were. Her list of your priorities had the job first, financial security second, the kids third, and your mom and dad fourth. She thought she came in somewhere after that."

Joe's first reaction was shock, then anger and defensiveness. Wasn't Teri right at the top of his list when he said, "family"?

"Not necessarily. I see men listing that a lot, but I say it can be a cop-out. For a strong marriage your wife should come ahead of the kids. You need to really think about the day your kids will be grown and gone. What will you and Teri have to talk about then? If Teri doesn't feel anywhere near the top of your list now, what will it be like later?"

Teri Had to Move to "Square Two"

Joe thanked me and went out. Now it was Teri's turn and we talked about her two lists of what was important—the one she'd made to represent her feelings when she first came to see me and the one that represented her feelings now.

"I'm glad to see you're getting time for yourself in the number-two spot, but I'm concerned about Joe in number four."

"Well, why not—I'm not even that high on his list, really."

"So where do you go from here? You're not high on his list and he's not high on yours. How can we change that? You *do* want to change that, don't you?"

Teri hesitated. "Well, I suppose I do. I've been feeling better about myself since I started coming to you for counseling, but Joe hasn't changed that much. He still works long hours and he's still not that involved with me and the children."

"I think it's time you went to square two.

What every woman wants to knows is, 'Does my husband love me?' You wanted to believe Joe when he said he was doing it for you and the kids. You figured that working all those hours was showing how he loved you. But when you got so stressed-out, you had to come for counseling. You had a chance to see things differently. Actually, you got permission, so to speak, to ask for a real marriage—to have a husband who is involved with you and the children—not just a good provider who is seldom there."

"Well, I suppose that's right. But how do we go to square two?"

"For you to go to square two means being more assertive in your marriage and playing a more active role. . . ."

"A more active role?" Teri sputtered. "I'm the only one who is active at all—I do the work while Joe lies around after dinner and complains about how tough it's been all day."

"I'm not talking about *that* kind of being active. You complain because Joe isn't very interested in you or the kids. When I talk about being more active, I mean *physically active.* I'm talking about showing more interest in Joe sexually."

"Are you suggesting I bribe him with sex?"

"Not bribe him; *attract him.* It's easy to write Joe off as a dolt and a drag, but it won't change him. You're waiting for Joe to change and suddenly become the husband and leader he's supposed to be. It won't happen. But you can change yourself—you can start treating Joe nicer, sympathizing with him about the pressure he's under. He *is* under pressure and he's trying to be the best husband he can."

"It sounds as if I am doing all the giving. . . ."

"Somebody has to make the first move. Maybe that's what Jesus meant when He talked about turning the other cheek and doing for others as you'd have them do for you. And I believe He even washed some feet to model what He was talking about."

Whenever I give women like Teri my "turn the other cheek and wash his feet" advice, I realize it sounds chauvinistic—even unfair. I admit that's possible. But I also know that it works and women are far more capable of doing it than men. I believe women are closer to life and their own emotions—and they can be great teachers of their husbands!

The Simple "Secret" to Reducing Stress

Teri and Joe Make a New Start

Teri decided to try my idea. For starters, she did what I suggest to many women: Kidnap your husband and take him away. The very next week Teri packed a picnic basket, picked up Joe from work, and went up to a lovely canyon and mountain area where they had dinner together on a blanket beside a stream.

In those peaceful, quiet surroundings Teri found enough courage to tell Joe exactly how she felt. She poured out her heart and told how wretched she was feeling about herself, their relationship, and the problems with the children. She admitted that she no longer believed she was a priority in his life, and what she wanted more than anything was to feel prized and needed by her husband. It seemed to her that everything else was more important to him, and she pleaded with him to join her in concentrating on the truly important things.

Joe was totally bowled over in more ways than one. He was touched by Teri's concern and asked her to forgive him for the way he had been acting. That was the start of a whole new life for both of them.

Over the next weeks and months, positive changes started happening in the relationship between Teri and Joe. He started making Teri feel more loved and prized. He even started helping a little bit after dinner instead of collapsing on the couch and rising at 11:00 P.M. to wink at her provocatively.

Meanwhile, Teri continued to take some time just for herself with aerobics and other activities each day. And she also continued working with her own children.

One of the things I helped Teri build into the family routine with her children is what I call Reality Discipline. She became proficient at holding her children accountable for their actions so she didn't always have to be on top of them, scolding and nagging and reminding them to do their chores, to be home on time, and so on.

For example, when one of the children didn't do a chore, she would simply hire someone else to do the job for the child and pay for it out of that child's allowance. This got their attention in a hurry! Teri told me she was amazed as she began to see that she didn't have to do everything for everyone—there was a simple and healthy way for her to be an authority without having to feel responsible for everybody else's actions and attitudes.

There was one more area that helped bring Teri and Joe into a new oneness with each other. During the first three years of their marriage they had worshiped together, but when their first child was born things became more hectic, and somehow they got away from the church. As Teri put it, "God seemed to have gone out the window of our lives."

I explained to Joe and Teri that it's quite typical to discuss physical and emotional problems, but we can't forget we are tridimensional beings. Besides the physical and the emotional, we have a spiritual side to our lives. I suggested that they make a commitment together to try to find a place of worship where they could feel comfortable and then faithfully attend as a family.

"One of the healthiest things you can do as a family is worship together. I don't know of a better way to start communicating to your kids about what you think is really important in life."

Joe protested slightly and mumbled something about "hypocrites in the church." I countered by admitting there *were* hypocrites in church and I couldn't think of a better place for them to be—they might even learn something. Anyway, would they give it a try?

Our talk hit home with Teri and Joe. In fact, the timing was perfect because already their little eight-year-old daughter, Tami, was starting to want to dress and look like a six-teen-year-old, complete with lipstick and long earrings! Teri and Joe were just starting to experience what all parents go through sooner or later. Their children were being influenced by the outside world—particularly the media. They were seeing that if parents don't get involved with their children's lives and start setting examples for them, things get out of hand rather quickly.

There is a lot of discussion today about teaching values, or what some call "values clarification." I think a lot of it is bunk. You really don't teach values to children; children absorb your values as they look up and see how Mommy and Daddy act toward each other, and as they see what is really important to their parents.

The Simple "Secret" to Reducing Stress

Teri and Joe Learned the "Secret"

The ending to the story of Teri and Joe is a happy one. I wish all the endings to my counseling stories were as nice. Joe and Teri rededicated themselves to each other, to their children, and to God.

Joe made tremendous strides in learning that his first responsibility is to his wife, then his children, and then to his job, financial security, and jogging. And Teri knew he meant it the day he came home to tell her he had cleared his schedule and would stay with the kids all afternoon so she could go out to do whatever she liked.

As for Teri, she got her stress under control. More correctly, she learned to *prevent a lot of her stress,* and she did it by discovering one basic secret. Throughout the story of Teri and Joe I have referred several times to the simple secret of preventing stress. That secret is *priorities.* If you can get your priorities straight, you have the foundational tool you need to control the pressures and tensions in your life and to prevent stress from becoming overwhelming and debilitating. When I share my little secret with people, I often hear them say, "Is that *all? Everybody* knows *that!?*"

I understand their response. It does seem overly simplistic to say, "Just get your priorities straight and you will handle stress much better." But according to the people who troop through my office for counseling, they may think they know this little secret, but they don't practice it very well. In fact, I would say the vast majority of families in America operate without a good understanding of how to order their priorities correctly. And that is why they live in a constant state of stress—the Swamp of Life, as I call it.

The best way I know of to get out of the Swamp and stay out is to use your slide rule—your priority system—to measure how you are living. What is *really* important? Are you living that way?

A priority slide rule is a good little gadget to carry around in your head. When people hit you with requests to serve on this committee or that, take out your slide rule and say, "Well, I'll have to think about that. I'll talk it over with my husband and children and get back to you."

And when the boss comes to you with a "great opportunity" for you to work longer hours or take on a job that means more time away from the family and far more responsibility than you know you can handle, take out your slide rule and review your priorities. It's amazing what this little tool can do to help you control stress in your life.

I admit it isn't easy. In fact, the easiest thing to do is leave your priority slide rule in a mental drawer and forget to use it. Life is just too full of exciting, tempting, and trying situations, particularly when you share it with several other people called "a family." We have already noted that children are Stressor Number One for many mothers. Now we need to take a closer look at why this is true and what to do about it.

6

Which Kids Cause the Most Stress?

"Tell me, Dr. Leman, is it okay for my twelve-year-old to read *Playboy*?"

In my work as a therapist and counselor I find three kinds of children: Attention getting, powerful, and avenging.

Children all start out as attention getters, a perfectly normal and natural trait for any child. When a child gains attention in positive ways—by being obedient, getting good grades, and so on—parents have no problem and there is no stress to speak of. But when a child gets attention in negative ways, then the stress can begin.

Which Kids Cause the Most Stress?

I tell mothers how to recognize the difference between a negative attention getter and a powerful child by checking the emotions they are feeling and expressing in response to the child's behavior.

If you are feeling annoyed and saying things like, "Buford, stop that! You are driving me bonkers . . ." you are dealing with an attention-getting child who usually ceases his antics when you ask him to—at least temporarily.

If you are feeling pushed and challenged and saying things like, "What did you say? I'm the one who's in charge here . . ." then you are dealing with a powerful child. You feel you need to show the child who's boss!

I do most of my work with moms who have attention getters or powerful children. Occasionally, however, I see parents who are feeling hurt, who are saying, "How could he do it to me?" When a parent has a child who consistently creates that kind of emotion, she is dealing with what I call the "avenging child."

The avenging child is past wanting to gain attention or power. He wants revenge. He wants to hurt people back for what he believes they have done to him. I have seen this kind of youngster walk into a room and join a group of his peers and within minutes have everyone angry, upset, and against him.

Avenging children usually don't emerge until teenage years. Very rarely I will run into a child as young as eight or nine who can be classified as an avenger, but normally they are far more likely to be in high school or beyond. Our correctional institutions are full of avenging children. Chronologically they may be adults, but emotionally they are still children. They want to "get back" at someone because they believe life has kicked them squarely in the teeth and they want to return the favor!

Let's take a look at these three kinds of children to see how dealing with them can cause stress, and how you can prevent it.

Little Bradford Gave His Mother No Peace

Suzanne, an attractive twenty-nine-year-old mom, came to see me with her four-year-old son, Bradford. Little Bradford was a sight to see: color coordinated from head to toe, with shiny new saddle shoes and the cleanest face I've ever seen on a four-year-old in my life.

When Suzanne and Bradford entered my

office, it took me about twenty seconds to
guess what the problem was. Suzanne took a
seat on the couch and her little four-year-old
proceeded to burrow himself into her rib
cage. If Bradford had gotten any closer to his
mom, he would have been on the other side of
her! Bradford's eyes never left mine and he
looked at me as if I were "the enemy."

If my initial impressions were correct,
Bradford was a clinging, whining child who
wanted sole possession of his mother and all of
her attention. I decided to test my observa-
tions, and at an appropriate point in our conversation I asked if little Bradford would like
to go out in the lobby and look at some of the
children's books and try out the gum ball machine.

Little Bradford made himself even smaller
and wouldn't move. Suzanne was trying to be
polite and courteous to show me how soft and
loving she could be with her little attention
getter. But there was no way he was going to
leave her side. Finally, she got him on his feet
and tried to move him toward the door. Bradford dug his heels into the rug and practically
made tread marks as she pushed him along.

We finally got Bradford into the outer lobby
and I was able to spend a few moments with

Suzanne alone. Obviously, she was quite nervous about leaving Bradford alone out there and we had to cut our conversation short. One thing she said was indisputable: "You know, I don't get any peace. I get no time to myself."

I told her that I could understand that, and then I told her why. Little Bradford was in what I call the latter stages of attention getting and moving fast toward becoming powerful. He seemed to be a shy and even pitiful little fellow, but I explained to Suzanne that Bradford was doing a number on her. He felt he only counted when he was the center of attention—particularly hers. Attention getters like Bradford have to have Mommy or Daddy or both involved with them all the time.

It took me several sessions to help Suzanne see that she had to set some limits for Bradford. Here was a kid who had to learn that when Mommy and Daddy's door is shut, he does not enter without knocking. Bradford had to learn that he couldn't cling to Mommy's legs all the time because that didn't feel good to Mommy and she would have to pick him up and take him to his room for a period of "time out," when he would sit on a chair or on his bed until he could come back and behave. Suzanne had to teach Bradford that his mom needed some space; she couldn't have a ball and chain on her leg everyplace she went.

Suzanne learned fast and, fortunately, so did Bradford. Perhaps one strong motivation was that Suzanne was seven months pregnant and she was realizing that in just a couple of months she would be going through the tremendous stress of bringing another child into the world and caring for a newborn. Actually, Suzanne's visit was perfectly timed. Even before she brought Bradford in for that first appointment, she had already made the choice to not be a slave to her four-year-old. She knew that things would have to change.

Bradford didn't go down without a battle. But as Mom set some guidelines and stuck with them, he finally gave in. By the time the baby was born, his behavior had improved 180 degrees. The key to Suzanne's success was that she stopped giving Bradford an audience. We'll see the same principle at work when we talk about the powerful child. The whole idea in dealing with the attention getter is to tell him in so many words, "It is really nice to have you around and I really do enjoy being with you and talking to you. But what I can't take is the constant whining, pleading, and asking to be picked up and held. That's when you have to go to your room so Mommy can have some time to herself."

Notice, if you please, the basic principle that I had Suzanne use. In order to avoid stress with little Bradford, she had to go back to Square One, which is labeled "PRIORI-TIES." Her major priority could not be little Bradford and letting him control her life and literally hang on her leg or burrow in her rib cage everywhere she went. She had to realize that for her sake and for his, he needed to be able to function independently and she needed some time for herself.

Wendy Was Running Her Little Brother's Life

You can spot controlling attention getters very early on. One of my clients was Wendy, age four, just about the cutest little girl you ever saw. She had a little brother, Andy, age three. Every place that little Andy went, Wendy was sure to go, with her arm around him, marshaling him through life. She got everything for him, she talked for him. If I tried to ask Andy a question, Wendy would answer it.

Wendy was a classic example of a typical little first-born child who was growing up to be a controller and a caretaker. On the surface it looked as if Wendy was a very conscientious, caring big sister, but it didn't take me long to spot a budding problem. Wendy was literally running Andy's life, and their parents hadn't really realized it.

The reason I got to see Wendy and Andy was that their parents had come for help with communications problems in their marriage. After getting those straightened out, they decided to have me check out their children, particularly three-year-old Andy, who still wasn't potty trained and was rather slow in general—with his speech, for example.

No wonder Andy was slow to talk. His big sister did all his talking for him! I helped Wendy's mom and dad realize that they had to get Andy some breathing room. Wendy was eventually going to psychologically cripple him by not letting him do anything for himself.

So we developed one-on-one times for each of the children, Mom taking Wendy and Dad taking Andy for special treats like breakfast, lunch, a trip to the zoo, and so on.

We also laid out a game plan for when the entire family was together. Mom and Dad learned to lovingly correct Wendy and tell her to back off in order to give her brother a chance to choose, go first, and in general, speak and do for himself.

Not only did the new arrangement help Andy but it greatly reduced stress for Mom and Dad as well. Little Wendy was actually running Mom and Dad, as well as Andy! The parents had sensed something was wrong, but could not put their finger on it.

"Your problem is that you have put both your kids at center stage," I explained. "Everything revolves around Andy and Wendy, and you don't even take time to do things just for yourselves. In a family, children should be Number Two, not Number One. Your marriage should come first."

Mom and Dad got the point. They realized that their "children first" attitude had left them wide open for the power plays of their little controller, Wendy, and the antics of Little Andy, who was "being slow" to get his share of attention. They lined up a caregiver and made it a ritual to get out by themselves at least one night a week, something they enjoyed immensely once they realized Wendy and Andy would do just fine without them for a few hours.

Let me repeat: All children are natural attention getters. The ones who can develop problems are the little Bradfords, who love to cling and not let Mommy go for any reason; the little Wendys, who want to control and be pleasantly bossy; the little Andys, who are easily led and need to be "stood on their own two feet," to face the world and make their own decisions.

There is a fine line between the attention getter and the powerful child. I've already mentioned how you can know when the line has been crossed. Instead of just being annoyed by negative, attention-getting behavior, now you are provoked. You are starting to mutter things like, "Who does this kid think he is? Only one of us is going to run this house and it's not going to be him!"

Little Missy Practiced Tantrum Power

When little Missy's parents brought her in to see me, they described her as "very sensitive." In fact, in the entire four years of her life she had been so sensitive that Mommy and Daddy could never leave her alone.

"You mean you can't leave her with a sitter when you go out for the evening?" I queried.

"No, I mean that when my wife wants to leave to go to the store and I'm still home, Missy may get hysterical if she wants to go with her mother and can't."

"What does Missy do when Mom won't let her go along to the store and she's left at home alone with you?" I asked. I was already quite sure we had a powerful child on our hands, but I wanted to hear it from Dad himself.

"Well, I guess you could call it a temper tantrum. First she whines, then she screams, and finally she bites and kicks."

"I call that kind of behavior a 'power tantrum.' " I said. "What do you do when she acts like that?"

At this point Missy's mother broke in to explain, "We used to try to reason with her, but lately we are down to trying to spank her while she's flopping around on the floor or we yell and scream at her to try to make her behave."

Which Kids Cause the Most Stress?

"And the reason you brought Missy in is because of the temper tantrums?"

"Well, not exactly," said Missy's dad. "What really bothers us is that lately she's begun to do a lot of lying—she's misbehaving in ways that have us really wondering what in the world is going on with her."

At this point I leveled with Mom and Dad and told them they had a powerful child on their hands. They had helped make her powerful and now they would have to learn to take some of her power away. One thing I have observed is that powerful children respect powerful adults. The problem was, Missy's mother and father weren't responding to her temper tantrums in a truly powerful way. They were coming down to her level, so to speak, and reacting to her with a tantrum of their own. I suggested that the next time Missy threw a temper tantrum in the home, the best approach would be to simply step over the child and leave her there screaming and kicking on the floor.

Mom was doubtful she could do that, but Dad was all for giving it a try. An opportunity came just a day or two later. Missy threw a power tantrum right in the hallway because Mom was leaving to go to the store and Missy couldn't go along. Mom stepped over Missy and left her there in the hallway, screaming and carrying on. Dad, who had also been instructed on what to do in this situation, calmly got out of his chair and told Missy he was going out in the backyard to work in his flower garden.

So there was Missy, lying in the hallway, crying her eyes out, screaming at the top of her lungs, while her mother went out the front door and her dad went out the back. Missy finally followed Dad out to the backyard and tried to get him involved in her plight with pleading and whining. Dad, however, pleasantly but firmly just kept potting some petunias.

How many times do you think Missy's parents had to take that course of action in order to get results? Missy stopped her temper tantrums almost immediately. Why? Because she no longer had an audience. There was no longer a payoff. As I recall, it took only two such incidents to stop a basic form of behavior Missy had been using on her parents almost from the cradle. Even infants have a sixth sense about how they can control their parents, and Missy had been doing a classic job of it for practically her entire life.

Which Kids Cause the Most Stress?

Missy had grown tremendously powerful and was used to having Daddy sit down with her when she threw a temper tantrum because Mother was leaving. She was used to having him say, "Now, honey, calm down. Your mother is going to be back in just a little bit, and she might bring you something from the store." And when Dad left, she would pull the same behavior on her mother.

Of course, all this placating of little Missy solved nothing. When one of the parents did bring home a little something from the store, it only encouraged Missy and rewarded her for her power tantrums. And when frustration drove Missy's parents to spank her and shout at her to get her to be quiet, that likewise drew a blank.

What brought results was refusing to play Missy's power games. The adults started acting like adults and began perceiving Missy as exactly what she was: a four-year-old who liked to misbehave to get her way. They stopped perceiving her as a threatening source of stress, and the stress level in that home went down remarkably.

How to Create a Powerful Child

Twelve-year-old Lance was one of the most powerful kids to ever enter my office. Physically, he was quite small and unimposing, but emotionally he was "Mr. T." His mother brought him to me out of sheer desperation.

I already knew, from previous discussions with Lance's mother, that he sassed her and used four-letter words that are commonly heard in locker rooms and bars. Lance was also a reader of *Playboy,* and worse. His mother didn't seem to have a clue as to how to handle him. She had come alone to our first counseling session and at one point had asked me, "Dr. Leman, what do you think? Is it all right for a twelve-year-old to read *Playboy?*"

"What do *you* think?" I responded while trying to maintain my therapist's neutral cool.

"Well, I guess it isn't very good, but with the way things are going today . . . I really don't know if it's okay or not!"

I spent the rest of that first session trying to assure Lance's mother that parents are still in authority over their children, despite "the way things are going today." Parents should never let something like the New Morality or the New Wave or the New Age intimidate them. One of Mom's biggest problems was that she had no help from Dad. He had always seen raising the children as women's work. I told her we would have to accept that for now and do the best we could with Lance. Why not bring him in?

Lance and I had a bit of trouble establishing a relationship. When I did not show shock or intimidation at his choice of vocabulary, he just got up and took off. He ran out of my office into the parking lot—with Mom in hot pursuit. I walked out to where Lance was making his last stand and gave him a choice:

"Look, you can stay out here and call our appointment off, but if you do, you pay for the appointment out of your own pocket."

I took quite a chance telling Lance that he, not his mother, would pay for the appointment. In the first place, I hadn't checked with her. In addition, I wasn't even sure Lance had any money of his own. But I was fortunate on both counts. Lance's mother and I had talked enough beforehand to establish a trusting relationship and I could see she was willing to cooperate. When Lance looked at his mother as if to say, "Do I have to pay?" she nodded grimly, and Lance did have a savings account with just enough in it to cover the one-hour appointment.

It was a turning point. Lance wasn't about to fork over his own precious cash to some flaky psychologist. He gave in and came back inside. It took several sessions to get *anywhere.* As I talked with Lance and his mother —separately and together—I got a classic lesson in how to build a powerful child. Start with a passive father, who never got involved with Lance or any of his brothers and sisters. Add a pleasing mother, who did the best she could with a very permissive style of parenting, and you have a tailor-made situation for a powerful little guy who sensed he was in charge practically from the beginning of his life.

At eighteen months of age, Lance refused to take a nap and would scream and fuss until his mother lay down on the rug with him, where he would fall asleep with his fingers entwined in her hair (just to be sure she couldn't get away). If she tried to slip away after he fell asleep, he would usually wake up and scream some more. Lance refused to sleep in his bed; he preferred the floor, the couch, anywhere but where Mom wanted him.

So, at eighteen months, Lance was in charge and it went downhill from there. By age twelve he was a powerful package indeed, who had his mother right on the edge of going bonkers.

I can't say we did wonders with Lance, but Mom got a lot of help. She admitted she had read too many "meet their every need and don't foul up their little psyche" shrink books. Throughout the counseling, which lasted eight months, Lance's mother learned to use Reality Discipline methods to keep her powerful son in line. As I will explain in chapter 7, Reality Discipline is simply making children responsible for their own actions, calling them to account for what they do and say. I used Reality Discipline on Lance in the parking lot when I gave him a choice between coming back inside and agreeing to counseling or paying for the one-hour appointment out of his own pocket.

During the time I counseled Lance, I had the dubious honor of applying Reality Discipline in a very real way. He was in sixth grade at the time and throughout the school year he had been getting failing grades. Lance had "blown off" school and was refusing to do what he was told. He also had problems with all authority figures in general. As the end of the school year approached, I advised his mother to keep Lance back, even though the typical approach taken in most schools is to pass the child on because he has "grown a lot socially."

"The worst thing you can do for Lance right now is to let him be promoted to seventh grade," I told his mother. "If you let the educators intimidate you at this point, good luck. You are the parent and you have a right to insist that he be held back."

Lance's mother decided to hold him back, but she didn't quite have the nerve to tell him. I was the lucky one who was elected to do so at our next counseling session. Here sat this powerful kid, staring at me with eyes full of hate, but they filled with tears when he got the news. Interestingly enough, this was another turning point—a break-through, as a matter of fact. One thing about powerful children is that they respect power. Lance had refused to meet his responsibilities at school and he paid the price. He didn't forget that and, while he didn't become any paragon of perfection, he did settle down to where at least he was civil to his mother and his brothers and sisters. He even started doing a little homework!

As you can see, there are all kinds and degrees of attention-getting and powerful behavior. When powerful behavior gets totally out of hand it can turn into the "avenging child." In the next case studies you will see a child somewhere on the borderline between being powerful and avenging. And you will also meet a teenage girl who has stepped over the line to get revenge against her father.

Jimmy Was Ripping at More Than the Furniture

I never had the opportunity to counsel ten-year-old Jimmy face-to-face, but I did hear about him in a letter his mother wrote to me after reading *Making Children Mind Without Losing Yours.* She had gotten a lot out of my book, but there was one thing I had not covered: "How do you deal with a ten-year-old who makes a practice of ripping and defacing furniture and teaching his two little brothers to do the same?"

According to his mother's letter, Jimmy was bright, creative, and imaginative—a real leader at school. But ever since he had been a toddler, he had been destructive around the house. Jimmy's parents had tried everything, from reason and polite requests to spankings, groundings, and even making him write, "I will not destroy the furniture" one hundred times!

But it was all to no avail. Not only was Jimmy continuing in his destructive ways but he was also teaching his two little brothers to do likewise, and they were all becoming quite adept at lying to cover up for one another.

When I wrote back to the mother, my advice centered on the fact that while she thought she had "tried everything," the key was to stick with some form of Reality Discipline that would really impress Jimmy (and his brothers) and make them accountable and responsible for their actions. It was my strong suspicion that, while this mother had tried various methods of punishment with her boys, she had not embarked on a long-range strategy of disciplining them with firmness and love.

In the case of Jimmy, I can't help but wonder if he wasn't in the process of moving—at a very young age—from a powerful child to an avenging one. When a child habitually rips and defaces furniture at age ten, there are problems in his background that are unresolved. Actually, Jimmy needed professional counseling, and I urged the mother to get some in their community.

Laura "Got Her Dad Real Good"

Fifteen-year-old Laura was unmarried and eight months pregnant when her mother brought her in to see me. Laura's first words to me were: "I'm going to keep my baby and nobody's going to tell me anything different. I hope you're not going to, doctor, because if you do I'm going to walk right out of here."

I responded by explaining to her that my place was not to tell her what to do but to find out where she was and where she wanted to go in life. I soon learned that Laura's parents wanted her to give the child up for adoption, but Laura was determined to keep it. It was a classic power struggle. Laura was more than a powerful child. She was getting revenge—particularly on her dad.

Laura's father had been detached from her life from the day she was born. He saw parenthood as women's work, and literally let his wife do it all. But she nurtured the children, disciplined them, got them off for school, took them to church, attended their games and functions, while Dad simply put in his time down at work and in front of the TV set.

I've mentioned the importance of a girl's relationship to her father and what can happen if that relationship isn't a good one. In Laura's case, there was no relationship. As I talked with Laura, it all came out: the hurt, the bitterness, the pain. At one point I asked her, "Tell me the one thing that would really get back at your dad—if there were one way, how would you get to him?"

Laura looked down at her swollen body and then up at me with a little smile playing on her lips? "Well, I guess I did a pretty good job, didn't I?"

Laura was like many teenage girls I see. They engage in promiscuous sex and get pregnant—all to "get back at Dad." They become avengers against hurts and wrongs they believe have been done them in the past. In this case, Laura sought attention and "love" from young men as a substitute for the love she didn't receive from her father.

The teenage years are typically the time when the avenging child emerges. Our prisons are full of people who have gotten revenge, first against their parents, perhaps, and then against society. Talk to the prisoners in any penitentiary and, invariably, you'll discover their family life was wanting in some radically serious way. They were reared by parents who used one or all of three kinds of parenting styles that can easily produce powerful or avenging children. Those three styles are:

AUTHORITARIAN
PERMISSIVE
NEGLECTFUL

Authoritarianism is long on use of the rod and harsh language and short on kindly encouragement and affection. Telltale comments by authoritarian parents who wind up in my office wondering what to do with their "incorrigible kids" sound like this:

"I know what's best for her, but she just won't listen."

"He'd better do it or else—as long as he lives under my roof, I'll make the rules!"

Permissiveness goes to the other extreme and is long on what parents perceive to be "love" and short on firm direction and guidelines. Telltale remarks by permissive parents who come to see me sound like this:

"Well, I believe in loving my children—if I love them hard enough, everything will turn out fine."

"I try to give my child everything he wants and needs. I think that's what a parent's job is all about."

Neglectful parenting is a third style that is not as prevalent as authoritarianism and permissiveness, but it's still out there. Neglectful parents are just that—they simply don't have much to do with their children. I've already mentioned several cases where the father in the family was actually being "neglectful" while still maintaining a respectable facade of "providing for his family" by working long hours. But in a truly neglectful situation, the parents simply aren't there. They virtually let the kids run loose and provide for themselves. Neglectful parents have an excellent chance of producing children filled with the need for revenge. Quite often inmates in penitentiaries had neglectful parents.

What, then, is the answer? What style of parenting can work to produce children who are givers and not takers, who are accountable and responsible, not rebellious and powerful?

I believe the answer lies in developing a style of parenting that is a balance between gentle but firm control and genuine love. How do we keep that balance when stress piles up like dirty laundry? With a tool I have already referred to, and which we'll now look at in a little more depth. If there is any real answer to preventing stress while raising your kids, it lies in learning and using the principles of Reality Discipline to train up your children in the way they should go. In the next chapter, I'll show you why.

7

Are You Raising Takers or Givers?

"For the past three years . . . I have said things like:

'Wait a minute, aren't I the parent?

Who's in charge here, anyway?

Oh, oh, here comes another phase!'"

Almost every day I get letters like this one:

> When Timothy was born my husband and I had been married for three years, were twenty-six years old, and both had the attitude we were "ready and prepared" for parenting, or so we thought. I have

to laugh now when I look back at our "nothing to it" attitudes. For the past three years I have been trying (more like running against the wind) to keep up with the growth and changes that Tim has been putting us all through. I have said to myself things like: "Wait a minute, aren't I the parent? Who's in charge here, anyway? Oh, oh, here comes another phase! Could he possibly still be teething? Dear Lord, HELP!"

Problems with rearing children are nothing new. They've been around since Adam and Eve struggled with raising Cain and Abel. Down through the centuries, parents have tried pleading, permitting, and punishing. They have decreed, demanded, and despaired.

As one woman put it, "I used to be a great mother—what's happening to me?"[1]

It is really no surprise that the most popular books I have written both deal with trying to stay sane while the kids have other plans for you. My first book promised *Parenthood Without Hassles (Well Almost)*. Next came *Making Children Mind Without Losing*

Yours. That phrase struck a chord with a lot of parents who were at Wits' End Corner until they tried what I call Reality Discipline.

I will share a few basics on Reality Discipline later in this chapter, but first we need to understand why children are such a primary source of stress and what parents can do about it. One thing they're doing about it is to stop having children. An interesting—and discouraging—statistic being tossed about by the experts is that 25 percent to 40 percent of women born in the 1960s will remain childless. For some, the reason is pursuing a career. Others fear bringing children up in a nuclear age. But I have a hunch that for many it's simply an admission that they don't want the hassle. They have watched their own parents struggle with child raising, and perhaps they have friends with children. They can see that parenting is a ticket to chronic, unrelieved stress.

Another current phenomenon is what *USA Today* calls "one of the fastest-growing segments of the population"—namely, career women who are waiting to have children until they are well into their thirties.[2] The good news for these women who have put aside children while pursuing a career is that when they do start a family they will be more mature and able to cope with frustration. The bad news is that they will have less energy and possibly be more rigid in their thinking, which will make them less patient with the rigors of motherhood.

Parents Push Their Kids Too Far Too Fast

One reason children become sources of stress is the perceptions of their parents. Mom and Dad see their child through eyes that are full of expectancy. And they often expect their children to "be just like them." Ironically, as I counsel families, I find that parents are more likely *not* to get along with the children who are most like them.

But the expectations remain and proliferate. The moment little Buford lets go with his first wail, his parents start fantasizing about his public-speaking abilities and dreaming of how he is going to be different from all the other kids. Their expectations for Buford tempt them to push the little guy too far too fast. Not only do his parents become overstressed but so does he.

Indeed, psychological research is starting to

confirm that Buford and his mom represent substantial numbers in the ranks of the over-stressed.

Stanford researcher Carl Thoresen, highly respected veteran professor of psychology and education, believes that 25 to 30 percent of children are "really under the gun." According to his findings, highly stressed children show a great deal more of the chronic symptoms of stress: headaches, sore throats, stomach problems, trouble sleeping, muscle tension in the neck and head, dry mouth, and sweaty palms.

Those same studies describe many women as suffering from sleep disorders, sexual dysfunction, pervasive feelings of anger, and a nagging sense of always being behind schedule.[3]

Are the children doing it to Mom, or is she doing it to the kids by expecting too much of them and herself? It could be a little bit—maybe a lot—of both.

A book I recommend all parents read is David Elkind's *The Hurried Child,* which has the very accurate subtitle "Growing Up Too Fast Too Soon." Elkind is a child psychologist and chairman of the child study department at Tufts University. He has been studying children for over half a century and believes that a major phenomenon of the last twenty years has been the subtle and not so subtle pressure parents put on their children to perform.

Elkind has seen the pendulum swing from the spoiled children who came out of the permissiveness of the fifties and sixties to hurried and stressed children who are being asked to grow up too fast, ". . . pushed in their early years toward many different types of achievement and exposed to experiences that tax their adaptive capacity."

He believes that, "just as, at bottom, spoiled children were stressed by the fear of their own power, hurried children are stressed by the fear of failure—of not achieving fast enough or high enough."[4]

I agree completely with Elkind when he talks about dressing our children like miniature adults and treating them the same way. Today I see mothers who have two-year-olds in gymnastics programs. Six-month-old babies are in designer clothing. I recently heard of eight-month-old babies who are being subjected to flash cards by moms who want them to get an early start in learning how to read!

All of this pushing kids out of the cradle too soon results in a giant paradox. Parents shake their heads over grade-schoolers who start talking and acting like teenagers as early as age eight or nine. What do parents expect? They've been pushing the kids to cope with challenges and pressures far beyond their years ever since they were babies.

I've found that fourth grade is something of a dividing line that brings real change in most children. A transformation takes place that I describe as a kind of "mental/emotional puberty." The peer group starts to become all-important. Little eight-and nine-year-olds become very aware of what other people have in terms of things, money, status.

One mother told me she noticed her nine-year-old son sinking lower and lower in his seat as they pulled up to the curb of his upper-middle-class school in their 1971 Plymouth. "What's the matter, honey, don't you feel well?" she asked. Almost in agony, little Steven replied, "Mom, I don't want to be *seen* in this car . . . it has black-walls and four doors!"

Then there was the mom who told me her daughter said, "Are you really wearing that blouse *outside* where people will *see* you?"

Are You Raising Takers or Givers?

Your Teenager Faces Heavy Stress

You would think that with all this pushing and shoving to achieve more and grow up faster, children would be ready and raring to go when they arrive at those two most stressful places of all: junior high and high school. Unfortunately, for many kids the exact opposite is true. I bluntly tell parents that by the time their child hits adolescence, he or she had better be good at something, or the pressures and temptations of life will be tremendously difficult.

I'm not saying a child has to be a genius, beautiful, possessor of a 4.0 grade point average, or blessed with the moves of a professional athlete. What I mean by "being good at something" is that the teenager has a sufficient amount of self-esteem that comes from his or her achievements, being a part of something that counts, and so on. For some, it could mean being part of a team, or perhaps playing the flute in the orchestra. For others it could be having lots of friends, or a job that provides money for clothes and extras. The key to self-esteem is that the teenager feels loved, accepted, and capable.

One of the most dynamic changes of life

comes as children begin the teenage years. I refer, of course, to physical puberty, which sees the biological clock inside of the child setting off a whole new myriad of drives, desires, and demands.

I know a parent who came around the corner and caught his thirteen-year-old daughter smiling (braces and all) into the mirror with different poses, turning her shoulders this way, propping her head that way, and primping her hair to "look just right." This thirteen-year-old is no different from millions of others who have collectively spent uncounted centuries in front of the mirror with comb and other beauty tools in hand.

Wanting to look good to attract the opposite sex is an innocent and wholesome desire, but it all turns sour when a teenager gets introduced to sex too fast and too soon. You haven't known heartbreak until you've talked to a fourteen-year-old girl whose body becomes a mass of oozing herpes blisters during her menstrual period. In another case, I recently counseled a youngster who had her first sexual experience at age twelve in the laundry room of a boy's home, while both his parents were in another part of the house.

Are You Raising Takers or Givers?

Are Your Children Learning to Be Givers or Takers?

One of the questions I ask parents is, "Are you raising a giver or a taker?" With all this tendency to push kids to grow up too fast, they learn to be far better at acquiring, collecting, and achieving for themselves than they are at serving, sharing, and giving to others. Where did the kids learn this? From the major models in their lives: their parents.

I will have a lot more to say about working moms in chapters 9 and 10, but it is worth noting here that the current practice of having both parents work in order to maintain a "good standard of living" is only one more factor that encourages families to pressure their children to "grow up fast."

While counseling, I might ask a working mother, "Do you really want to watch your children grow up?"

The mother responds, "What do you mean? Of course I'm watching my children grow up —I don't have much time but I do the best I can."

"I understand your problem," I respond, "but it's all a matter of priorities. Do you want to be an integral part of your children's lives?

Do you want to be close enough to know how they think and feel? Or do you want someone else to do that for you?"

When children are small, that "someone else" is a caregiver—a baby-sitter, a nursery school worker, a preschool attendant, possibly a grandma. As the children grow older, that someone else becomes the peer group. Parents of teenagers in senior high school admit to me that now they realize the stress and pressures of rearing children through the preschool and elementary years is mild compared to keeping track of a sixteen-year-old with a brand-new driver's license and a taste for fast cars and a fast crowd.

High school brings pressures from every direction: drinking, eating disorders, drugs. Promiscuity calls from all sides. For teenagers who manage to stay out of that kind of trouble, there are still the very real problems of just growing up. How do you preserve self-esteem when your grades are dropping, your popularity is falling off, and life looks about as attractive as the new zit that just popped up on the end of your nose before the big date on Saturday night?

Something I suggest to parents of teenagers, and which I'm starting to practice myself with my own children, is to get to know the kids they associate with. Invite them to the house and be there to provide plenty of food, friendliness, and acceptance, along with just enough supervision to let them know you care.

A good part of my counseling case load has to do with situations in which parents weren't around to supervise teenagers. They had copped out to pursue careers or their own social lives, and excused the whole thing by saying, "Teenagers don't want adults around anyway."

What does all this tell a teenager except that his parents want him to grow up fast and not give them any trouble? Through their own self-centered behavior, parents teach their kids to become takers instead of givers! It is no mystery why teenagers often give their parents all kinds of hassle. It's as if they are trying to say, "You pushed me to grow up fast and be independent. So here I am, doing just that. How do *you* like it?"

How to Raise Givers Instead of Takers

All parents like to recall situations or events that were good learning experiences for their children. One of my own favorites is the time my oldest child, Holly, and her fifth-grade classmates provided food and other practical gifts to needy people right in our community.

What made the project so valuable, however, was their "hands-on approach." Instead of just collecting money and having the teacher send the check to some agency that could in turn help these less-fortunate people, Holly and her friends took the food and other things to their homes and handed it to them, eyeball-to-eyeball, so to speak. Holly will never forget standing in the kitchen of a grateful mother who seemed to have at least a dozen kids. The floor was clean, but it wasn't made of tile, hardwood, or linoleum. It was *bare dirt*, and as Holly visited that modest dwelling she got an education in cultural differences and sociology that no textbook could ever provide.

I believe experiences like that are what produce a child who is a giver, not a taker. What do I mean by "givers and takers" and why is it important for stressed-out mothers to know the difference? I can think of several reasons:

- Givers understand reality and human need.
- Takers prefer fantasy and meeting their own needs.

- Givers want to be accountable, responsible citizens.
- Takers really don't want to account to anyone or have many responsibilities.

- Givers realize they may have to wait to get what they want or even do without.
- Takers live by the law of instant gratification.

I could go on, but I think you get the idea. When I talk about givers versus takers, I am not trying to build a lecture or sermon on how to be a "goody-goody." I am really talking about giving children a basic foundation for life that will show up in all kinds of ways when they are grown and raising families of their own. For example:

- Givers stick with a marriage when the going gets tough.

- Takers bail out because they aren't be-ing "fulfilled."

- Givers look out for their families.
- Takers look out for themselves.

- Givers parent their children with re-spect and fairness.
- Takers parent their children without really considering their personal worth and opinions.

In my opinion, there is no better proving ground for detecting the attitude of giver or taker than the family. And to all stressed-out moms I'd like to make one thing clear: When I talk about "giving" I don't mean playing the part of maid, doormat, and slave while your husband and children go their merry "tak-ing" ways. If you want your kids (and maybe hubby, too?) to learn how to give a little, they need training and instruction. They need liv-ing, breathing examples of how it all happens.

They need Reality Discipline.

I'll admit I'm a bit prejudiced about how useful Reality Discipline can be. Most psy-chologists have their own philosophy of child rearing, and I'm no exception. But the reason

I am so high on Reality Discipline is that *I know it works.*

If parents—especially moms, who usually get the brunt of child rearing—will use Reality Discipline methods consistently, they may not eliminate stressful problems completely, but they can prevent the pressures and subsequent stress from slowly driving them bonkers.

Why Is Reality Discipline So Wonderful?

To explain Reality Discipline completely would take an entire book, and that's what I tried to do in *Making Children Mind Without Losing Yours.* Ever since writing that book, however, I've had one problem with the title: To rear a giver, not a taker, you don't *make* a child mind; you *give* the child opportunity to choose and make personal decisions. You give the child freedom to fail as you teach responsibility and accountability. When you use Reality Discipline.[5]

> 1. You don't seek to punish; you look for ways to discipline, train, and teach.
> 2. *You* don't cause the "punishment," pain, or consequences the child may

have to face; *reality* causes the pain or consequences as your child learns how the real world works.

3. You don't swing back and forth between permissive (too much love and not enough control) one minute and authoritarian (too much control and not enough love) the next.

Some psychologists describe the middle ground between too much love and too much control as "being authoritative," meaning that you are in charge but still reasonable, fair, and loving. I've used the term *authoritative* myself, but I like the idea of "balance" better. And there is no better tool to achieve the best balance between the two extremes than Reality Discipline.

4. You teach accountability and responsibility in a way that helps your child learn as he makes his own decisions and experiences the consequences of his own mistakes and failure, along with his own successes.

In short, when you use Reality Discipline, you allow your child to become an individual with a self-image that allows him or her to function confidently and unselfishly. There is a great deal of talk today about building confident children who have adequate self-esteem. My office is full of children (and parents) who are battling serious self-image problems. Reality Discipline can do a great deal to build self-esteem, but for best results it should be used from the cradle on.

For example, don't be afraid to leave your child with a trusted baby-sitter and go out for the evening. This way the child learns the world doesn't revolve around him. Also, there's nothing wrong with using a playpen. Kids have to learn that Mom's responsibilities go beyond entertaining the eighteen-month-old. It's much easier to bake a cake or balance the checkbook without a little one wrapped around your ankle.

How Reality Discipline Works in Practice

Whether I'm advising parents one-on-one in my office, or talking to a group of them at a seminar or convention, I try to emphasize that Reality Discipline is not a gimmick or the magic answer to everything. To paraphrase an old saying, "Reality Discipline works if you do." Here are some basic principles to follow as you teach your children to be giving and loving, not taking and selfish.

Always make your child responsible and accountable for his actions. Takers have little or no sense of responsibility or accountability. They are too busy thinking about Number One. Givers have learned from their earliest years that everything they do or don't do has a final result and consequence.

Suppose, for example, Mom tells four-year-old Harold, "It's time to pick up the toys. We have to leave for our doctor's appointment."

Little Harold whines, "I can't, they're too heavy!"

Mom says nothing, and takes Harold to the appointment. On the way home they pass an ice-cream stand and Harold wails to stop and get an ice-cream cone. Mom drives right on by, saying, "I can't turn the steering wheel, it's too heavy."

If Mom hangs tough and does not give in to Harold's pleas and whines, he will get the message. He will learn, "When I pick up my toys, I get a treat. When I don't, no treats!"

Are You Raising Takers or Givers?

At the grade-school level, opportunities to teach "natural consequences" are everywhere. If the child breaks a toy, he buys a new one out of his own allowance. If the child doesn't get up when Mom calls him for breakfast, he misses the school bus and has to walk to school and face the consequences of being tardy and explaining why to his teacher, or the principal.

At the teenage level, you can help your young person face responsibilities by letting him pay his own traffic tickets and standing up in court alone, if he has to go to court. A battleground for most parents and teenagers is "curfew hour." If you want to use Reality Discipline in regard to curfew, try this:

Explain to your teenagers that being late will mean forfeiting use of the car (or some other coveted privilege) for a week (or whatever amount of time you agree upon). When your teenager leaves for the evening, have him set an alarm clock for the agreed-upon curfew hour and leave it within earshot of your bedroom. The teenager knows that not getting home in time to shut off the alarm will mean two things:

1. His parents may be awakened out of a sound sleep and be quite perturbed.

2. His parents, who may be lying awake worried sick, will know the precise moment of truth regarding the breaking of curfew.

Either way, there will be no guessing or arguing. The teenager set the alarm himself, and it was his responsibility to be home in time to shut it off.

You may, of course, choose to make a deal with your teenager and ask him to phone if he can't get home in time through no fault of his own: a flat tire, or a change of plans by others that he can't control. The key to making curfew (or any other rule) work is to be friendly, fair, and *firm.* Once the alarm goes off, there is no weaseling out of it. The consequences must be paid.

Be consistent. Takers have little self-discipline because their parents are inconsistent and undisciplined themselves. Givers are far more likely to come out of a home in which discipline is firm but always fairly enforced.

The key to success is to not use Reality Discipline and then slip back into permissiveness or authoritarianism on another occasion. There will be many difficult moments when you have to back up what you have said as the consequences for certain behavior. Your child will test you to see how much he can take in a given situation. With Reality Discipline, you can teach him he has to give instead.

For example, from infancy on, the child should have a consistent bedtime. You might allow your child to "stay up late" on special occasions, but be sure the occasions are very special and very exceptional.

One of the best ways to teach consistency is with the clock. Suppose your child ignores the rule to be home by six o'clock for dinner. He "forgets" or just plain stays out longer because he was having such a great time. The rule is simple: No dinner. I often find mothers who cringe at this idea and argue vehemently with me about being unloving and too severe. My answer is that I have never known of a child who died from missing one meal, or even several. If you are consistent with your dinner-hour policy, the child won't miss very many meals. (Also, make it a point to call your children *only once* for dinner.)

It gets harder to be consistent when your child reaches junior high and high school, but it still pays off. I have already given one example of how to be consistent regarding curfew. I always advise parents to not see the day their teenager gets a driver's license as one of impending disaster. On the contrary, it gives parents tremendous leverage. Driving is a privilege that few teenagers look upon as minor or unimportant. To "have wheels" is crucial for a teenager. Once he breaks an agreed-upon rule and must pay the consequence of not driving, the parent should never relent (not even to let him run up to the store for a loaf of bread). Let me add here that Reality Discipline works far better with a teenager if that child has been reared with Reality Discipline from an early age.

Always teach your child to delay gratification until responsibilities are met. Takers put personal plans and desires ahead of responsibilities every time; givers make sure their responsibilities come first. For example, even a toddler can learn that, "first we pick up our toys, then we watch 'Sesame Street.'" A grade-schooler is far better equipped for life when he learns that chores come before fun—even Little League!

At the teenage level, instant gratification is almost a cult ritual. In many instances, your best weapon here is your checkbook—keeping it in your desk, that is. Teenagers have to have the new jacket, new glove, latest whatever, *now.* Life is moving fast. All the other kids have one, and if they don't get one *now,* they will simply die.

The parent who can practice Reality Discipline in the face of this kind of powerful argument first outlines the reasons the money isn't available. Then, if the teenager insists that he or she will die without the desired object, the parent simply says, "You will not die, but you must face reality."

Another obvious answer for the teenager who "just has to have" that certain something is to suggest that he earn his own money and buy it himself. When the teenager works for money outside his home, he is far more appreciative of what that money will buy.

Another way to teach your child accountability, along with learning to delay instant gratification, is to allow him to be involved in the process of paying the bills each month. This may be "a lot of extra trouble," but it could be well worth it. You may want to wait until the child is a certain age to trust him with this kind of information, but I really believe that even twelve- and thirteen-year-olds are quite capable of taking part in knowing how the family budget actually works, and, by trusting the child with this information, you show him respect. As your child learns the realities of keeping a family going, he learns that he may have to put off certain things, wait, and "save up" for something he feels he has to have.

And, there is one other possible benefit to letting the child help "pay the bills." If he learns the realities of how much it costs to run a family when he's as young as twelve or thirteen, he is much less likely to drop out of school when he's sixteen to take a job that will get him nowhere. He will be much more likely to finish school and get the education he needs to earn adequate money to live on.

Treat your child with respect—never with sarcasm, arrogance, or "talking down." Takers have little respect for others because they have never learned how to treat others respectfully. Givers learn respectful behavior best from parents who have modeled it for them. In other words, people who grow up to respect others have been respected themselves in their own homes.

I have seen mothers of Little League baseball players yelling at their eight-year-old sons as they stand trembling at the plate, "Put your hands together, Billy. Move them up on the bat, you dummy. Spread your legs apart."

Are You Raising Takers or Givers?

I'm a baseball fan myself, and in one instance when this went on I could not contain myself. I tried to say something to the mother, and she told me in no uncertain terms to mind my own business!

Something else you must realize is that you can show a small child respect by "getting down to his level" to talk to him. Consider how you would feel if you had to go through life straining your neck muscles to talk to giants who were anywhere from fifteen to twenty feet tall! We could paraphrase the old saying this way: "No mother ever stood so tall who stooped to really talk to her child."

At the adolescent level, respect really becomes a crucial issue. Remember that you don't demand respect from a teenager. You earn it. Do you allow your teenager privacy? Do you take his or her problems seriously, or do you just laugh and say, "Oh, you'll get over that—I had to when I was in high school."

Reality Discipline—Is That All There Is?

I can understand if some mothers are saying at this point, "Is this guy Leman trying to tell me that all there is to parenting is learning how to discipline my kids correctly?"

Obviously, there is a lot more to parenting than that. What I just covered barely scratches the surface of how Reality Discipline can relive and prevent stress in parenting. To be a parent is tough enough under any circumstances, but to be under constant stress because you can't solve the problem of finding the happy medium between being too tough or being too gentle is foolish—and unnecessary.

I realize that by talking about Reality Discipline I may sound like a commercial for *Making Children Mind Without Losing Yours,* but I'll take that chance. Frankly, if you're a mom who is feeling the pressures and stress of parenting, I urge you get the book and read it carefully. It is loaded with practical tips that I don't have room to share here. Reality Discipline can help relieve stress caused by children who are . . .

. . . talking back or tattling on each other.

. . . in potty training or under peer-group pressure.

. . . forgetting to do their chores or forgetting "what time it is."

. . . failing to get up in the morning or fighting to stay up every night.

. . . lacking the necessary motivation to follow through on chores, school assignments, and other responsibilities.

Also keep in mind that as you seek to train up children who are givers and not takers, there will be moments when they do cross over and take rather than give. All of us do that every day. The goal is to develop an attitude toward life that is more giving than taking.

Whatever you do, remember, *you don't have to be a perfect parent.* In fact, you will be a more effective parent if you can realize how imperfect you really are! Even Reality Discipline won't work perfectly every time. If you can learn to relax and accept the calamities and head-on collisions with reality, your stress level will go down and stay down.

Obviously, the person who needs Reality Discipline the most is *you.* But you don't help yourself toward stress-reducing self-discipline if you try to be Super Mom. In the next chapter I'll introduce you to some Super Moms and give some suggestions on how to become an "average, ordinary mother" who may not always have it all perfectly together, with every hair in place, but at the same time is happy to be a mother because you know where everything is—especially your priorities.

8

Help! I'm a Cabbie and My Minivan Isn't Even Yellow

Super Mom meets the enemy and "She Is Me."

Meet Marge, who arrives at her first counseling appointment with her three children in tow. Her problem? The children are incorrigible and she is exhausted. Marge has that certain look, so I ask her what kinds of activities her three children are involved in besides school.

"Well, Stephanie is thirteen and she plays Bobby Sox Softball, takes ballet and tap dancing, and is also very active in the young people's group at church. Bobby is eleven and he's playing Little League right now, and in the fall he plays soccer. He also takes guitar lessons, is a Boy Scout, and just last week he started bowling with a team from church. Kristi is nine and she's in Brownies and takes gymnastics. I'm also thinking of starting her on piano when she turns ten next month. Like all of our children, she is quite musical."

Marge is the kind of mother I call a "cabbie parent." She keeps busy driving her kids from here to there and back over there, and then across town again. When you mix all of her children's activities with her own—president of her women's club, a deaconess in her church (she's also taking tole painting lessons one night a week)—you have what is politely called "an overextended situation." To put it simply, Marge and her kids are running themselves ragged.

Next meet Elaine, age thirty-one, mother of two small children and holder of a full-time job as office manager in a large manufacturing company.

There was no question Elaine was competent, but as we talked I detected the hard-driving Type A personality that never relaxed and was always impatient—everything had to be perfect. Elaine came to each session with a list of things she wanted to talk about, and we always ran out of time. We never covered all of the things she wanted to discuss. It struck me that she probably did the same thing at her office and at home.

I asked her if she was a list maker and she admitted she was. "Yes, lots of lists." She even had lists to find her lists. Lots and lots of lists were part of Elaine's life. I asked her if she would mind bringing in one of her typical "to do" lists to our next counseling session. She said it would be no problem and, sure enough, the next week we started off by looking at Elaine's "to do" list for that very day.

I took a good look at the list, which seemed inordinately long.

"Now tell me, is your list of things to do *today?*"

Elaine nodded her head yes, so I asked, "What are the chances of getting through all these items today?"

"On, none. There is no way I could ever get through that entire list."

"Then why do you have the list labeled right here at the top, 'Today's to Do List'?"

"Hmmm, I really don't know," was all Elaine could say.

Let's leave Elaine for the moment and

meet one more mother, who has a three-year-old and another child on the way. Delores came to me with all kinds of physical symptoms: severe headaches, always feeling tired, occasional backaches, and ringing ears. Her family doctor had called it "hypertension."

"Why did you come to see me?" I asked.

"Because I feel so guilty. I'm so fatigued and frustrated that I resent being a mom. I resent having given up the good job I had before Billy came. Now I have another child on the way and I am resenting that."

"And all this resentment is what makes you feel guilty?"

"Yes . . . I shouldn't feel guilty. I shouldn't resent being a mother; I should be happy that I am blessed with a healthy little boy and that this pregnancy's going so well. But I get irritable, I fly off the handle with Tom, and I cry over nothing. The other day I cried because I couldn't find the mint jelly at the supermarket."

"Fatigue can make anyone irritable," I commented. "Are there any other reasons you are so short of temper?"

"Well, when Billy was born, I committed myself to being the *best* mother I could possibly be. I wanted to do everything right. I wanted to be there when he took his first steps. That's why I quit work. I've read just about every child-rearing book on the market. I just know I'm not doing it all as well as I could. I should be a better mother, but I'm so *tired.* . . ."

The Super Mom Syndrome Is Practically Universal

And so there you have them: Marge, the cabbie; Elaine, the list maker; and hypertense Delores, who is guilt-ridden because she "should be doing a better job." What do these three women have in common? We could make quite a list ourselves, but I would like to boil it down to one basic problem: They all suffer from what I call "Super Mom Syndrome," a condition familiar to most wives and mothers to one degree or another.

As a matter of fact, my personal hunch is that all mothers have Super Mom tendencies —those yearnings to step into a phone booth (more likely, it's a broom closet), and reappear as a "caped crusader" who is faster at getting her kids to school than any bus and stronger than any man when it's time to wipe

up the real messes in the middle of the night
—the one who leaps insurmountable problems at a single bound as she loves and pro-
tects her family.

And how long will Super Mom last? Just
about as long as her energy does. Hans Selye,
the pioneer researcher in stress whom we
talked about back in chapter 2, has some in-
sights on energy that are particularly apropos
to mothers. Anytime we undergo stress, we
move through what Selye called the General
Adaptation Syndrome in which the first two
stages are Alarm and Resistance. As we saw in
chapter 2, when we become alarmed by anything that may produce fear, pressure, or tension, our adrenaline starts to flow and we are
prepared to resist. In Selye's classic terms, we
usually try "fight or flight." All of this takes
what Selye called "adaptation energy." The
interesting thing about our adaptation energy
is that *it is limited*. We have only so much, and
when that is gone, we enter Selye's third
stage of the General Adaptation Syndrome—
Exhaustion.

When mothers like Marge, Elaine, and
Delores come to see me, they are well into
the Exhaustion stage. In fact, they are well on
their way to what is popularly being referred

to today as "burnout." In an excellent book
entitled *Parent Burnout,* Joseph Procaccini
sounds a lot like Selye when he says your most
precious resource as a parent is your energy,
but *your energy is limited.* To avoid burnout,
you must control—and conserve—your personal energy supply.[1]

According to Dr. Procaccini, the Super
Mom who is headed for burnout has the following characteristics:

- She has a list of *shoulds* that are unob-
  tainable. (Remember Elaine, our list
  maker?)
- She feels responsible for things that
  might happen to members of her family, even though she has no control over
  those events (in other words, she feels
  guilt-ridden, much as Delores did).
- She treats everything that happens as a
  "federal case"—a major issue that is absolutely crucial.

This last characteristic is called "crucializ-
ing"—worrying so much about decisions that
their importance is blown completely out of
proportion. The mother wonders if she should
have done more breast-feeding, should have

read more stories with her child, should have taken more time to listen, should not have gone back to work so soon, and so on.[2]

Why All Moms Are Burnout Prone

All three of the above characteristics are deadly. But perhaps the most dangerous is the classic Super Mom feeling that she is responsible for the happiness and achievements of everyone in her family. Feeling responsible for things over which you have no control is a sure way to put yourself under tremendous stress. To put it in Selye's terms, you use up your adaptation energy in a hurry and soon find yourself exhausted or "burned out."

One client told me, "I feel so responsible. I even feel responsible for the rainy weather we had while my relatives were out here visiting from back East!"

I realize that some mothers will say. "That's not me. I don't have the hang-ups that Marge, Elaine, or Delores have, but I'm still tired and frustrated a lot of the time."

My answer is that there is a multitude of ways to suffer from Super Mom Syndrome. I believe there is a conspiracy of sorts against every woman who becomes a mother. By the very nature of the task, she becomes burnout prone. Consider the job description: on call twenty-four hours a day, seven days a week, for eighteen (or more) years.

Just ask the children. They instinctively know that Mom is far better equipped to meet their needs than Dad is.

No one is as soft and cuddly as Mom.

No one understands the way Mom does.

No one can fix things or find things the way Mom can. It's not that kids have anything against Dad—they just know where to go when the chips are down.

I have personally experienced the phenomenon of sitting right next to my children as they scream for Sande, saying, "Mom, where are my white shoes? Where's my green hairbrush?"

Do the children not see me, their father? Of course they do, but somehow they intuitively know that Mom is the one they must talk to about these urgent matters.

And, or course, Mom responds. It's no wonder Mom is tempted to do it all; she winds up doing most of it anyway.

Super Mom Goes Shopping

In the last few weeks, while finishing up this book, I saw a simple but powerful example of Super Mom at work in our family. We traveled from Tucson to Phoenix for the weekend with several goals in mind. I am a totally committed fan of all University of Arizona athletic teams, and I wanted to see the Cats rip Arizona State in baseball. Sande wanted to get some shopping done at an especially famous discount house that had excellent buys on clothes. The kids just wanted to have a good time in the motel pool and any other place that presented possibilities.

We got in on Friday night and watched the Cats lose a slugfest 12 to 9. The next morning Sande, Holly, our oldest daughter, and I went out shopping. I won't describe the day in great detail. All I will say is that Sande ran my legs off. We went to what seemed like a dozen stores before arriving at the famous discount establishment. By then it was late afternoon and I was begging for mercy. Sande kept saying, "Just five minutes more."

Fifty-five minutes later I dragged myself out the door behind her, trying to peer over the packages to find the car. She had tirelessly searched for all kinds of bargains for kids' clothes and had also picked out several shirts for me. (Why do I let her pick my shirts? Because I am as color-blind as a saguaro cactus.)

Our Phoenix shopping expedition is a simple illustration of how the same experience can be fun and beneficial for one person and unpleasant and stressful for another. While shopping, Sande and I both used up some adaptation energy, but in her case she was under just enough stress to accomplish her goals and have a good time doing it.

We had hurried out that morning to be sure we got finished with everything on our list. (Yes, we did make a list.) And we succeeded (except for not being able to find fourteen-year-old Holly just the right bathing suit). Sande used up some of her adaptation energy, but she enjoyed it. All day long she kept saying, "I love to shop!" And who was she shopping for? Kevey, Krissy, Holly—and me. She loves her family and loves spending her time and energy on us.

As Selye points out, there is no point in hoarding your energy and not spending any of it. Life demands that we put ourselves under some stress or we would accomplish nothing and have no fun. In Selye's words:

173

In terms of the adaptation energy consumed by the stress of life, the secret of success is not to avoid stress and thereby endure an uneventful, boring life, for then our wealth would do us no good, but to learn to use our capital wisely, to get maximal satisfaction at the lowest price.[3]

And so our trip to Phoenix was a good example of Sande spending her energy wisely and getting maximum satisfaction while doing so. She had a great weekend because she did something she loves. As for me, the weekend was not quite so much fun. The Cats dropped two out of three games to our arch rivals, the Arizona State Sun Devils. The shopping exhausted me, and on the way home our car had some "falling apart" problems.

"Okay, Famous One, Take Out the Garbage"

Our adventures during the weekend in Phoenix were just a tiny glimpse of how life can be an enjoyable challenge or a stressful drag. Sande can shop all day; I'm exhausted in seventy-five minutes. Fortunately, I'm not on call to go shopping very often. And when we got back to Tucson, I wasn't on call to do more shopping, plan dinner, take Holly to youth group, put in another load of wash, take Krissy to softball practice, deliver something for the "Women's World" group, and be sure that Kevey gets to his Little League game. Even though we try to limit our kids to only one or two special activities each, the Super Mom schedule piles up for Sande, too.

With all this discussion of Sande's busy schedule, you may be wondering if Dr. Leman pitches in at home at all. Quite a bit, as a matter of fact. If I don't, I get one of my books quoted back to me in no uncertain terms. Being an author has its moments of excitement and even grandeur, but my family isn't that impressed. There's nothing like hanging up from a telephone interview with a radio station or returning from a trip to be on a national TV talk show and have Sande say, "Oh, Famous One, take the garbage out now. . . ."

My point is that, while I try to pitch in at home, Sande still faces the Super Mom Syndrome and the constant threat of burnout. Like every other mother, she has "one of

those weeks" every now and then. Most
women can handle that kind of stress off and
on, but when stress piles up, their batteries
run down, exhaustion sets in, and burnout can
result.

One mom I talked to put her definition of
stress in this nutshell: "Feeling like I just can't
be all things to all people."

Another wife, who obviously didn't get that
much support from hubby, reached the point
where she said wearily: "Basically, I'm the
only one who works in the home. I feel responsible for three other humans" (her husband and two children, ages nine and five).

The Deadliest Enemy of Them All

Back in chapter 4 we went over the six biggest causes of stress in a woman's life: children, overloaded schedules, husbands, lack of
money, housework, and jobs outside the
home. So far we've touched quite a bit on
coping with the children, as well as with husbands who don't get very involved at home.
But perhaps the deadliest enemy of them all,
especially for Super Moms heading down
Burnout Trail, is the overloaded schedule.

Many women I counsel are like Elaine, the list maker we met earlier. These people are "discouraged or defeated perfectionists." They seem to carry around with them a little stick that I call the "high-jump bar of life." They never seem to be able to jump high enough over that bar.

Oh, there are times when they take a flying leap and manage to clear the bar, but then, guess what? They raise the bar still higher! Why? Because they know they "could have done better." Do they raise the bar a half inch or possibly one inch? Of course not; they figuratively raise the bar five or six inches, which usually programs them for failure, or at least more and more stress as they try to jump higher and higher.

I see a lot of self-defeating behavior in the Elaines of America. Ironically, this perfectionist tendency can usually be spotted at a young age. I see it in the child who starts a lot of projects but never finishes any of them. Or worse yet, she doesn't start them at all. Instead, she backs off from any kind of competition or pressure. She literally tells herself, "I'm afraid to fail—so afraid, that I will protect myself from failure by not trying." Then she goes on to tell herself another lie which sounds like this: "Well, I could have done it but I really didn't feel like it. If I had had more time, I know I could have done a great job."

This kind of person often grows up to become very critical. I refer to these people as the "flaw pickers of life." They can spot a flaw at fifty yards and are often found in quality-control positions on assembly lines. Being a flaw picker can be a tremendous asset if you're in an occupation that demands perfectionist precision.

For example, accountants, engineers, executive secretaries, and others, are paid to find flaws or avoid them. However, when they bring that critical, perfectionist nature home with them, the fur can fly. The wife who finds flaws in her husband soon has him finding flaws in her. And the mom who finds fault with her kids often winds up in my office wondering why her children are so critical and difficult to live with.

Moms who carry the burden of a defeated-perfectionist personality really don't need any enemies in life because they have all the enemies they can handle right inside their own skin. The perfectionist Super Mom could easily be caught saying, "I have met the enemy and she is me!"

Some other telltale characteristics of the perfectionist include a lack of being able to delegate responsibility, not being able to say no, and being overwhelmed by the big picture.

Which Kind of Perfectionist Are You?

I have counseled many Super Moms who can't seem to let go of some of their responsibilities. They complain bitterly about their work load, but if they do delegate duties—to their husbands, children, or possibly to some other member of the family or friends—they still tend to hang over that person's shoulder, checking on what he does and how he does it. Perfectionists have a driving need to do everything and be sure everything is "right." They over-plan and quickly become bogged down by having too many irons in the fire.

This "do-everything-myself perfectionist" tends to be a pleaser—she needs to have everybody like her. She wants to be all things to all people. A skill she lacks almost completely is the ability to say, "No, I can't."

Unfortunately, this kind of pleaser perfectionist often becomes overwhelmed by the big picture. She fails to see that anything—from a beautiful cathedral to a backyard barbecue—is built one brick at a time. This kind of perfectionist will whip out her "to do" list at seven o'clock in the morning and become overwhelmed because there is no way she can "get all that done today!"

The opposite of the pleasing perfectionist is the stressed-out workaholic whose life-style is strictly that of a controller. Whenever we hear the word *workaholic,* we usually think of men, but I see more and more women fitting the description. The workaholic seems to thrive on competition—especially with herself. She is often motivated by guilt and always has a need to control, win, and be the boss.

This kind of Super Mom is an expert at doing many things at the same time. She reads the paper, balances her checkbook, and gobbles down lunch, all in the same fifteen minutes. Her schedule dominates her life and she lives to complete every item on her "to do" list.

As we saw with people like Elaine, she has far too many items on that list and never gets them done. A typical lifeline perfectionists hand themselves is based on "all or nothing" thinking that has them saying something like this: "I got everything done on my list but two items. I'm a failure again!"

Or, perfectionists might overgeneralize, especially when they make mistakes. A typical line the perfectionist will hand herself when she goofs is, "I'm always fouling it up. I'll never get it right."

The third favorite lifeline of the perfectionist always contains the work *should,* which we've already discussed. The perfectionist lives under the "tyranny of the should." Whenever she falls short of a goal or makes a mistake, she doesn't ask herself, "What can I learn from this?" or "How can I avoid this problem next time?" Instead she says, "I should know better. I should be able to handle that. I don't dare do that again!"

Whether you're a pleaser perfectionist, a workaholic, or a controlling perfectionist, it's a stressful way to live. Not all Super Moms are perfectionists, but I meet many who show a lot of the signs. They are under tremendous stress, and they blame their schedules, the children, their husbands, their jobs, and so on. In truth, they should blame themselves.

It usually catches up with all of us sooner or later. It caught up with me, and I'll talk about that in chapter 11. The point is, we can't treat our bodies as if they were machines. To repeat Selye's principle, we have only so much adaptation energy. When it's out, it's *out.*

It wouldn't hurt a lot of us to say something like this each morning: "Be kind to yourself today. Don't bend, staple, fold, or mutilate!"

How to Lower the Bar and Your Stress

My advice to all Super Moms (and dads) is to lower that high-jump bar of life and quit whipping yourself to always set a new record. In fact, I suggest that you stop reaching for "super" and settle for "satisfactory" or maybe "above average." Not only will it greatly reduce stress but it will also increase your overall effectiveness and well-being. Following are some basic suggestions that have a proven track record with my clients.

We have already talked about the basic secret to avoiding stress: establishing priorities (*see* chapter 5). I also believe that every mother—particularly the working mother—

needs to become skilled at doing three additional things:

1. Take smaller bites of life.
2. Learn to say no cheerfully and without guilt.
3. Don't try to please everybody.

Obviously, all three of the above skills are linked inseparably to that "priority slide rule" I mentioned way back in chapter 5. Notice how each of the three tips are built on each other. Your first hurdle is to stop being a slave to your "to do" list and your schedule.

If you can decide that you must cut back and take smaller bites of life, the other two steps come much more easily. Once you are committed to doing less, saying no is not so hard. In fact, you will have to say no in order to carry out your intention to cut down.

And once your learn to say no, it won't be hard at all to learn that you can't please everyone. You will be able to live more happily with the realization that everyone on this earth does not have to like you.

How Marge Solved Her "Super Schedule"

For an illustration of how all this can work,
let's go back to Marge, our Super Mom who
drove her minivan taxi from one end of town
to the other, hauling her three children to
three or four or more activities apiece all year
long. Actually, I've seen parents worse off
then Marge. I've counseled families in which
each child was involved in as many as six
things: soccer, flute lessons, piano lessons, tap
dancing, ballet, gymnastics—you name it,
kids seem to want it, and Super Moms duti-
fully tool their minivans to the next appointment.

So what was my advice to Marge, who was
not only getting burned out energywise but
also starting to feel the pinch financially from
all the things the kids were involved in?
"Have everyone take smaller bites of life," I
told her. "Tell each child to reduce his or her
activities from three or four down to one, or
two at the most."

When Marge got that news, she gasped.
"But they'll all have a fit!" she protested.

"Oh, they'll holler, all right," I acknowl-
edged. "But just tell them they can't have
Disneyland every day. Kids simply can't go on

all the rides they want in life. It's not good for them. They need structure and they need limits. Besides, it's not good for you. If you don't set some limits, you will go bonkers, and soon."

"But how can I tell them?" she wailed.

"Well, the new school semester is starting in a week or two. Just announce right now that this coming semester they can only be involved in two things each, at the most. This will give them a little bit of warning and time to decide which activities to choose."

Marge left muttering, "How can this lead to less stress—sounds like *more* to me!"

But she took my advice and made her announcement. Of course the kids responded as predicted. They sounded like the packs of coyotes that we often hear yelping at night out behind our home here in Tucson. Marge's little pups didn't like her news at all. They thought they had a right to do all the wonderful things they had been doing before.

Yes, it's true that the first salvo of wails and complaints from her kids was stressful for Marge. But in the long run it was the kind of stress that was quickly over and quite beneficial. When the kids realized that Marge would not crack under their pressure, life became much easier and more peaceful for them all.

And not only did Marge spend less time in her minivan taxi; she and her husband spent less money because many of the things the kids had been doing were very costly. In the case of the youngest daughter, she loved horses and had her own horse. Since the family did not live in an area zoned for horses, she had to keep the animal on a farm several miles away. This meant that Mom had to take her ten-year-old daughter out to the farm almost every day to feed the horse, clean the horse, and ride the horse.

Because of the substantial amount of time and money involved with the horse, Kristi was given a choice: Keep the horse and have no other activity, or give up the horse and be able to do two other less-time-and-money-consuming things.

Because Kristi loved her horse, she opted for him, and learned a little in the process about priorities and how much things cost.

Perhaps you think Marge was too soft and didn't gain that much if she had to take Kristi out to visit her horse five days a week. In this case, Marge was willing to do it because she liked horses herself and the frequent trek to the farm was relaxing as well as a good time to build a strong relationship with Kristi.

As for the other two children, they were also put on a budget and could only spend so much time and money on their two allowed activities. After their initial griping and tears had subsided, Marge discovered a serendipity with some of the extra money realized from expenses. She was able to have her husband's shirts done at the laundry. That way she avoided a weekly chore that had been a source of stress in itself.

"You were right," she said at one of our last counseling sessions later that fall. "Resetting all of our priorities has made a difference. I still seem to do a lot of driving, but now it's under control."

Because I knew Marge was a first-born pleaser and something of a perfectionist, I asked her, "How are you doing with the perfectionism—the desire to cover all the bases and keep everybody happy?"

"It's been hard. It's been especially hard to say no to my children, but you're right. If I can hold my ground and even be willing to have them dislike me for a few days, it finally smoothes out. I notice the kids are happier, too. They were getting as stressed as I was."

Marge finished up counseling not long after that. I realize that telling her story in a "nice pat little case study" makes it all sound easy. It wasn't. I said it earlier, and I'll underline it again here:

GETTING YOUR PRIORITIES STRAIGHT AND STICKING TO THEM IS ONE OF THE MOST DIFFICULT TASKS IN LIFE.

Habits are hard to break; life-styles and lifelines are difficult to change. It usually takes running totally out of adaptation energy—reaching the Exhaustion stage of the stress syndrome—to get a person's attention and motivate real change. But until there is real change, all of the "relaxation response" techniques in the world won't solve your problem. I'm not against relaxation techniques and methods. In fact, I use several of them myself, which I will be sharing in chapters 9 and 10 when we talk about the working woman.

One of the most life-changing phenomena occurring in America during the last ten years is the number of women, especially the number of mothers, who are leaving home and their children to make all the ends meet. Obviously, the typical working mom is automatically forced into the role of playing "Super Mom." But her problems are special and we need to look at them in more detail.

9

Why Stress Stalks the Working Woman

"Circumstances pile up, I have no control, and people demand 'performance' from me."

Let's call her Nancy. I don't know her real name because she was one of hundreds of women who responded anonymously to our stress survey. Nancy is thirty-two, married, and struggling with all the pressures that come from rearing a seven- and a four-year-old. Her biggest source of stress? "Trying to stay a one-income family when the world's standard is two incomes."

I say "bravo" to this lady, and I hope she can keep going on one income, assuming, of course, that the one income is her husband's and that she is trying to stay home to cope with the kids and keep the house together. But while I'm saying "bravo," I realize she may be fighting a losing battle. There is a new kind of American family out there, and it features mothers who have joined dads in the work place. Some say it's for the better, but my counseling load tells me that in many cases it's for the worse—particularly if you're talking about preventing stress attacks and the disease I call "bonkers."

As I pointed out earlier, latest statistics tell us 56 percent of mothers with children under eighteen are working—full-or part-time. In addition, many of these women are single mothers, or part of a second, or even a third, marriage. The statistics also say only 14 percent of American homes are "traditional," with the couple in a first marriage, Dad going out to bring home the proverbial bacon and Mom staying home to tend the runny noses of the ankle-biter battalion.

Not that tending the ankle biters isn't work. As one mom wryly observed, *"All* mothers work. The lucky ones get paid!"

How lucky they are might be debatable, but there is no debate about today's economic realities. Many households need dual bread-winners in order to barely make it. A big item is housing. Some wives go to work to help find enough cash flow to float the new home that costs between twenty-five and fifty thousand dollars more than hubby's check can cover.

In addition, psychological realities find many women saying they want to get out into the work place to be "more than a house-wife." So the economic and psychological re-alities are out there, but so are the problems that come with Mom leaving home to gain a paycheck. I sympathize with working moth-ers because I know they are facing three big questions:

1. Who will care for my kids?
2. How do I cope with the guilt?
3. What about the strain on my mar-riage?

Granted, a lot of working moms don't have to contend with the third concern because they are single. We'll spend chapter 10 talking to the single mother, but right here I want to deal with the woman who is married, has chil-dren, and is working full- or part-time for any combination of reasons.

To put it in typical terms, imagine with me,

if you will, today's all-American couple: Ralph pulls down $40,000 a year with an aircraft company, while Betty brings home $29,500 as a marketing manager for a small dress manufacturer in town. They have two children, ages three and one.

Their house is in Marlborough Ranch, complete with "wooded-view lot, pool and Jacuzzi, gourmet kitchen with greenhouse windows, raised oval bathtub in the master suite, and a three-car garage."

The monthly payments, of course, are also raised, as are the payments on their two cars, a minivan, and a sports coupe. Let's look at their options, especially Betty's, as they face those three big questions.

Who Cares About My Kids (and My Guilt)?

It is fascinating to see how our terminology changes as the decades roll by. Back in the seventy's and sixty's and even earlier, we talked about "getting a sitter." Then it was "find a day-care center" or "enroll the children in preschool." Today the mother of small, or even not so small, children who wants to keep working looks for a "caregiver." The idea behind the term *caregiver* is easy enough to understand. When we are out working we want our children nurtured, supervised, and if necessary, disciplined in a loving but competent way. A caregiver is much more likely to deliver on all those counts than a baby-sitter or a preschool attendant.

I suppose I am from the old-fashioned school, but I have trouble with the way our psychological and sociological jargon adapts to the "needs of the time"—in other words, what people think they want. I've read that the "experts" are suggesting a parent should try to stay home at least four months with a newborn child before finding a caregiver and getting back to work. One reason for not getting back to work immediately is the need to "bond" the child to the mother.

Bonding is a psychological term that describes the building of certain emotional ties between mother and child that last for life. I believe bonding does occur, but I have my own term for the idea that you can bond your child to you in four months and then head out the door, briefcase in hand, confident that all is well. My technical description for this kind of thinking is "Baloney!" You don't bond a child in four months. You build ties with your children all through their young lives and up through adolescence.

So the obvious question is this: Can you go back to work and still succeed in building strong emotional ties through bonding your child? My answer is yes, if you work at it— very hard. The working mother may have to depend on someone to give her child care each day, but she never depends on the caregiver to become "mom" to her child.

Most mothers instinctively know this and that is why they wrestle so fiercely with guilt when work takes them out of the nest and leaves their fledglings in the hands of someone else. It may sound better to call that someone a caregiver, but Mom still cringes inside when she thinks about missing those golden moments like baby's first steps, or not being there to handle those less-than-golden moments when reality calls for some discipline.

There are a lot of books out there on "how to have it all, even if you're a working mother and have to go it alone." But what happens on those mornings when your child runs a temperature and looks at you with those droopy eyes as you start out the door and says,

"Mommy, don't leave. I don't feel so good"? There is no book that can untie the knots in Mom's stomach at a moment like that.

Of course, the pat answer is to call the office and say, "I won't be in today—my child is ill." If you're high enough on the totem pole, that may work. If you are not high enough, you may get fired and, even if you are able to "call in sick with your kid," you still struggle with guilt feelings in reverse. You're not keeping up with all the other working women down at the office who are also "after it all." In fact, some of them may be after your job! You don't want your boss to see you as an employee who can't be depended on to pull her weight because she is "encumbered" by children.

Just as an aside, let me say that the work place has yet to adjust to the changing family. Working parents would be less stressed if they could take advantage of innovations such as flexible hours, increased maternity and paternity leaves, and on-site child-care facilities.

Is the Jacuzzi Really Worth It?

It's easy to pick the working mom apart and leave her impaled on the horns of her guilt dilemma. But what are some practical answers she could use to prevent or battle stress? I have three suggestions:

1. priorities
2. Priorities
3. PRIORITIES

First, I suggest that the working mother take out her priority slide rule and think through just how necessary her job is right now while the kids are small. Are the pool and the Jacuzzi really worth it? Is there a way to cut down on clothes, entertainment, cars, and stay home, at least during these early crucial years when your child's personality, life-style, and lifelines are being formed?

Some moms are doing it. Three of them were described in an article in *Redbook* magazine, which asked its readers what they thought of a woman who believes she belongs at home with her child, despite the disapproval of husband and friends. For example, there was thirty-six-year-old Sandra, who quit teaching twenty-five kids in a classroom to spend more time with her own two children. Her son's temper tantrums subsided immediately and her daughter stopped wetting the bed, but her husband resented the loss of her paycheck and having to shoulder the entire breadwinner load. He started giving her sharp little digs such as, "Somebody around here has to make some money." While they were able to talk about it, the tension remained and Sandra still felt as if he saw her quitting work as a cop-out.[1]

Wouldn't it be great if some profamily tax reforms were instituted in our country? Some kind of tax credit for non-working (outside the home) mothers that would reward her and, in the long run, her family.

One of my clients didn't quit work altogether, but she did put priorities into action to solve her problems. Lucy, thirty-four-year-old mother of Lisa, age twelve, took a part-time job that paid fairly well, but it meant working afternoons when Lisa came home from school. To save on caregiving costs, Lucy let Lisa become a "latchkey kid" and, while she felt a bit guilty about not being able to supervise her daughter each day when she got home from school, she told herself, "Lisa's mature—she can handle it."

Things changed, however, the day Lisa got caught shoplifting. Lucy took out her priority slide rule and made some rapid computations. She felt she needed to work because she couldn't stay cooped up at home all day. But getting out of the house wasn't worth having her unsupervised daughter get in trouble. Lucy quit her higher-paying part-time job and took something that paid a lot less but allowed her to be home almost an hour ahead of Lisa each day.

Lucy's story illustrates how a simple change can solve a stressful problem. But it's amazing how many moms won't change. They prefer to keep bringing their children to me so I can "fix" them. What needs fixing is the parental priority scale. Changing your job, or your schedule, may not be easy, but it isn't as hard as having the police or sheriff call and say, "Mrs. Jones? We are holding your daughter because she was caught shoplifting. Can you come right down?"

A Short Course in Choosing a Caregiver

The stories of Sandra and Lucy illustrate some options for working moms to consider. But what about the working woman who can't quit her job or change it to one with more convenient hours? The house payment is not going away—in fact, at your house there is no pool or raised oval tub, but you still have to help your husband pay those bills.

I say the answer still lies in priorities. If you need a caregiver, make getting a good one a top priority. The better your child's caregiver, the less guilt you will feel.

In *Prime-Time Parenting*, Kay Kuzma's excellent book designed especially for families in which Mom and Dad both work, she includes a thorough discussion of how to find the best caregiver for your child. She lists the pros and cons of several alternatives in caregiving, including these:

- A live-in maid or relative who could be anyone from a full-time housekeeper to a graduate student exchanging room and board for being a help to you.
- A baby-sitter who comes right to your home, which is especially nice if you have younger children who don't like new situations.
- A family "day-care mother" who has a license to care for a certain number of kids in her own home.
- A nonlicensed situation in which you might go to a friend or relative who will care for your child in her own home.

- Another mother who will exchange child-care services with you.
- A group-care situation which could be anything from a nursery school to a preschool to a day-care center.
- A baby-sitting pool, which is like exchanging child care with another mother, only on a larger scale.
- A home play group situation in which you join with four or five other mothers who arrange morning and afternoon programs with the children, rotating to a different mother's home each day or week. This puts one mother in charge of all the children while the other mothers have some free hours. (This approach doesn't provide much help for the working mom, however.)
- A parent-operated cooperative nursery school or day-care program, which means each parent or set of parents must contribute a certain number of days of work or volunteer to help with other services (again, not too useful for working parents).[2]

In her chapter "Sharing the Child-Care Responsibility," Kay Kuzma includes a "child-care evaluation" checklist that contains some excellent requirements and standards you should be looking for (*see* page 209). In my biased opinion, the best kind of caregiver is a grandmotherly type who is willing and able to give your child the no-nonsense, loving touch he or she needs at this critical time in life. I believe we are missing out on something truly wonderful in our society by not making more opportunities for the very young and the older person to be together and fill important needs in each other's lives. It's true that the children need care, but the older folks need to feel needed.

If it works out to the satisfaction of all concerned, a grandma and grandpa can be a natural solution to your caregiver problems, but notice I said "to the satisfaction of all concerned." If you are living near your own parents or your husband's, it can be very tempting to ask Grandma and Grandpa to donate some free child care. Some grandparents are more than happy to help out a daughter or daughter-in-law who has to work. But other grandparents may feel that they have put in their fair share of years raising children, and they have some free time coming. Be sure to discuss all the ramifications thoroughly if you intend to use grandparents as caregivers while you work.

The reason you need to be cautious with the grandparents is that they come from another generation that has had a different value system. In many counseling cases, I find that grandparents are a primary source of stress and guilt for working mothers because "in their day they didn't do things like that."

The scene is not unfamiliar. Here is a young mother battling pressures to keep her job, keep her marriage relatively tension-free, keep the children clean, well-dressed, and educated. What are Grandpa and Grandma doing? They are busy tossing their harpoons of disapproval and judgment from clear back in Ohio by way of the mail or Ma Bell. (Some of Mom's *worst* phone calls are from a disapproving parent or in-law who can't understand why she has to go traipsing off to work and leave little Buford in the lurch all day.)

Your First Responsibility Is to Each Other

Disapproval from parents or in-laws can put real strain on your marriage, which may be reeling already due to your having to spend so much time out of the home at work. Surveys show that women actually work longer than men, and that leaves less time for everyone at home—especially hubby. By the time you pick up the kids from the caregiver, put dinner together, clean up, and put the kids to bed, there is not much time for romance.

If your husband has flexible work hours— suppose he sells insurance and he knocks off early to play golf—it can be a pretty tense moment when he sidles up around 10:00 or 11:00 P.M. asking if you "wanna fool around." No, you do not want to fool around. You are physically exhausted and ready to drown your stress in your king-size water bed.

Remember Teri, the Super Mom who worked part-time teaching fifteen preschoolers five days a week, and her husband, Joe, who worked overtime and didn't help much at home? The key to solving their problem didn't lie in Teri's quitting work (which she did). The key didn't lie in Teri's scheduling one fun activity just for herself (which she did). The real key for Teri and Joe was learning to put each other first on the priority scale. One of my standard pieces of advice to married couples under tension, pressure, and stress is to do what Teri and Joe did: Get away by yourselves, without the children, and have fun, communicate, make love.

"If nothing else," I tell such a couple, "just take an overnight in a nearby motel."

Strangely enough, it's hard to get people off their stress treadmills. They prefer to plod straight ahead toward exhaustion, burnout, and heart attacks. They tell me:

"We can't afford it."

"We both have jobs."

"We have responsibilities—besides, the children will miss us."

To all these profound protests I say, "Hogwash."

Money might be tight, but you can't afford *not* to spend some of it on relaxing and talking together.

You both may have jobs, but do you both work seven days a week? (If you do, something had better change, and fast.)

Yes, you both have responsibilities, but your first responsibility should be to each other. So the kids will miss you; it will be worth it when you return to them less up-tight and tense.

Chuck and Judy Brought in a College Student

The more a husband and wife can work together, the easier it will be to handle stress. For example, housework is a classic source of stress for the working mother. I often tell clients, "What does a working woman need when she comes home at night? A 'wife' to greet her at the door with a cup of coffee and a list of everything that's been done around the house." If a husband can be that "wife," all to the good, but in many cases the husband is still out there fighting the freeways himself. The working couple needs to prioritize and decide how to provide some hired help when it's necessary.

Chuck and Judy were both working and came to me for counseling because things were just getting "too tense." It didn't take long to discover that the evening mealtime was a main cause of their stress. To be frank, the period from 5:00 P.M. to 7:00 P.M. must have been like living at the circus. When Chuck wasn't working late, Judy took her turn to be late. The kids had different activities from which they needed to be picked up before dinner, and in a couple of cases there were different nights of the week when they had to be somewhere by 6:45 P.M. for clubs or youth groups.

My first suggestion to Chuck and Judy was to limit their schedules, but they didn't buy that one at all. They felt that everything the kids were doing was vital and well worth the hassle. So, I suggested getting some part-time help and, because I had connections at the University of Arizona Department of Home Economics, I managed to line up a nineteen-year-old sophomore who was willing to come to the home at 4:30 P.M. each day and be a combination caregiver to the three children and chief cook and cleaner-upper after dinner.

With the college student giving them this kind of help five days a week, Chuck and Judy were on Cloud Nine. Because both of them drew good salaries, money wasn't a problem. They were happy to pay the college girl quite well for her services, and she turned out to be great with the kids, plus a good cook!

In this case I was gratified to see that Chuck was willing to get Judy the help she needed. So many husbands would pinch pennies (and their relationships with their wives) by refusing to bring in a caregiver and trying to "get along on our own"—meaning, let the wife do it. Working wives whose husbands make them their Number One priority are fortunate indeed. As I often tell them, "If you have a good husband, hang on to him. They're hard to train."

Dr. Dobson Answers My Question

It's not hard for a husband to say, "My wife is Number One." I know a lot of men who are totally committed to that idea, including myself. But *making* her Number One is not always easy. Life—particularly the schedule—closes in.

I recall a conversation I had with Dr. James Dobson after being interviewed for his "Focus on the Family" radio broadcast. I had been doing too much traveling, had been away from home a great deal, and was starting to feel it, in more ways than one. I knew Jim had been over that same kind of road, so I asked him, "What advice do you have for me —a husband and father who travels the country, speaking at conventions and conferences, and who is away from home a lot?"

Jim didn't hesitate for a second. He said

"Kevin, before you do anything in life, run it by Sande first."

What Dr. Dobson was telling me was to make sure my wife is always part of my decisions. If the schedule piles up, she can be part of helping me decide what I can cover—and what I can't.

That's good advice for any husband to follow—or for any wife to practice with her husband, for that matter. When a husband and wife value each other by asking. "What do you think? Your opinion is important to me," two things happen. Instead of their marriage relationship being a source of stress, it is a source of strength. As they honor each other, both spouses gain new energy to battle the pressures and tensions they encounter each day at work, not to mention at home when they're with the kids, whether it's the "prime time," dinnertime, bathtime, or bedtime.

But what happens when you are a mother who has to go it alone, rearing the children and probably working full-time as well? I counsel many single women who claim they are glad to be shed of old Harry, because the relationship was destroying both of them. But as we shall see, single moms pay a high price for their "freedom."

Child-Care Evaluation Checklist

Type of Care

1. Does this care meet the current needs of my child?
2. Is it appropriate for his age?
3. How long might I expect this care to be appropriate?
4. Is this care the best for my own personal needs?

Caregiver

1. Am I convinced the caregiver is the best I can find for my child?
2. Is the person specifically interested in my child?
3. Has she established a rapport with my child?
4. Is she able to discipline my child in a firm but loving manner?
5. Does she support me?

6. Is she willing to talk to me about my child's progress as well as the problems?
7. Is she encouraging to my child, as well as to me?
8. Am I convinced she can act wisely in case of an emergency?

Activities

1. Are the activities my child is participating in appropriate for his age?
2. Is there adequate freedom within the environment so he can make appropriate choices to work or play with materials on his own time schedule?
3. Is he able to work at his own level of ability without any pressure to perform just like other children?
4. Is there a variety of activities and material available to encourage learning?

Environment

1. Is the environment wholesome, healthy, and safe?
2. Is good food served regularly?
3. Is there an adequate resting period that is encouraged but not forced upon the child?

4. Are there adequate emergency proce-
   dures?

Miscellaneous

1. Is my child happy and satisfied?
2. Does my child talk positively about child
   care?
3. Is he eager to go or accepting of the situation?
4. Are there any signs in my child's behavior that would indicate unhappiness:
   sleeplessness, excessive crying, regres-
   sion to immature behavior, excessive ag-
   gressiveness, destructiveness, listless-
   ness, a tendency to withdraw, nervous
   habits such as nail biting, twisting hair,
   and so on?
5. Are the children he is with the type of
   children I would want him to have as
   friends?[3]

10

Single Moms Carry a Double Load

"I get tired of being strong."

HAPPINESS IS BEING SINGLE. It's a familiar bumper sticker. Whenever I see it, I always wonder. *"Is* happiness being single?" Growing numbers of women seem to think so. They have had it and want out. They are seeking freedom from all that stress and pain. And after they get out, are they relieved and at peace? Not as a rule.

We also have to keep in mind that many women didn't choose to become single parents. Some of them are widows; quite a few were divorced by men who went seeking "greener pastures." Whatever the case, single moms carry a double load.

When I asked her to describe causes of stress in her life, a thirty-two-year-old mother I'll call Marsha told it like it is: "What is stress? It's single parenting, feeling stuck financially, bored with my present career. I've been single for the past ten years and see no change ahead. I'm afraid of being alone, of growing old alone. . . ."

And how does Marsha react to the pressure of being a single mom with all these feelings —*plus* having a fifteen-year-old daughter? She added: "I sometimes ignore my teenager. I just don't want to deal with all the problems. . . ."

And the the capper—Marsha's final cry for help before caving in? "I get tired of being strong."

Advice to the Single Mom: "Don't Panic"

Much of what we have covered for married working women is equally useful to single mothers who are trying to raise their kids and hold down a job as well. Single parenting has its own problems, however, and some special areas in which I try to help the single mom include the following:

1. *A single mom should never try to be a dad.* I advise single mothers to not go out and buy a glove so they can play ball with their sons. A mother should be a mother, and if at all possible obtain "male input" for her children through grandfathers, uncles, or other male members of her family, if the children's father doesn't play an active role in their lives. If this won't work, try your church to see if there aren't men who would give your children some time. Big Brothers is a well-known organization that might be another answer.

My point is this: *No one can play the part of both parents.* You will be far more help to your children if you are *yourself* and you strive to be the best mother you can be under the circumstances.

2. *Make finding a good caregiver your top priority.* Review the material on caregivers in chapter 9, and also note a word of advice: Make a special effort not to impose on relatives, friends, or neighbors who are "stay at home" mothers (meaning they don't work outside the home). With all her pressures, a single mom might be tempted to think, *It's*

*okay to ask Eleanor to watch my kids. She at
least has a husband—and she doesn't even
work!*

While that kind of reasoning might be logi-
cal to a harried and hassled single mother, it
could be a fast way to lose friends and upset
in-laws. The following letter, from a woman
in Texas, was written in answer to a nationally
syndicated "Working Woman" columnist who
advised mothers of latchkey kids to not be shy
about asking stay-at-home moms living
nearby to take responsibility for their children while they are at work. Approximately
one hundred mothers wrote in with a similar
response, but the irate Texan's words are particularly worth reading. She says:

> I'm reading your column on kids
> . . . and I'm amused that despite all
> the liberation in the world, you're
> still relying on *mom* to cover your
> bases. Oh, not the kids' mom, of
> course—just whatever at-home
> mother happens to be in your neigh-
> borhood.
>
> On a television show about moth-
> ers and the work place, several
> months ago, the commentator began

the special by calling the stay-at-home mom "extinct."

Now, by my arithmetic, half of all women are still at home. At the very least, we're a very strong minority. But the corporate princesses of the media, it would seem, prefer that we not exist at all.

Until they want our help, of course.

I always get a good chuckle when an emancipated mom, putting on airs of self-sufficiency, relies on her *own* mom or mom-in-law to raise her kids. Or pays disgracefully low wages to some vulnerable woman to take over.

Success seems to mean that instead of being exploited, a woman gets to be the exploiter. "Making it" means making another woman do your dirty work. An interesting little class struggle, don't you think?

I used to feel supportive of my working friends—until their babies came. Then our friendships began to be strained because I refused to be their "mom."

They put my name and number down at the day-care center for emergencies—without asking me—but the real clincher was when they expected me to be their backup baby-sitter when their arrangements fell through. And they frequently did.

What really got me was their assumption that I was at their disposal because they were in the work place. They knew my time did not belong to the company, so they assumed it belonged to them!

I never cease to be amazed at this sense of entitlement. There must be some peculiar glitch in the psyche of a working mom that allows her to believe that every at-home mom is at her beck and call. What's your explanation?

But then, you support such attitudes in your column, don't you? Elementary-age latchkey kids can rely on the mom next door, right?

Although we live in a society where there's a lawsuit around every corner, you encourage women to expect that a neighbor will take responsibility for a household emergency.

There are many at-home moms who won't say no to you—women who feel guilty about refusing responsibility are not found exclusively in the work place.

But the simple facts are that I take care of *my* kids, and I don't owe working moms any free services. It isn't necessary for me to "have it all," and I don't see why I should strain to make it possible for another woman to.

Frankly, this guilt you working mothers try so hard to avoid seems rather well-placed. If I found out about a second-grader left to her own devices from eight in the morning to six at night, I'd call the local child-abuse authorities. In my neck of the woods, it's illegal.

There is an ever-widening rift between at-home moms and women in the work place. Telling working women to dump on a neighbor won't do anything to lessen it.[1]

Bonkers

Single working moms reading the above may wonder if I'm just trying to increase their own load of guilt, but not so. The stay-at-home mom from Texas is coming down a bit hard, but she makes good sense, and I simply pass her letter along as a word to the wise. Even if it costs more in time or money, live by this motto: "There is no free caregiving." You'll be happier; so will your family, friends and neighbors.

Now let's get back to those tips for single moms:

3. *Be a strong disciplinarian.* I counsel many single mothers who are at their wits' end because they can't handle the children. A mother can do a great deal to help her sons grow up to be better candidates for marriage if she will not take any guff from them. Review chapters 6 and 7 in this book, and put Reality Discipline to work in your home in earnest.

4. *Avoid "triangles."* I don't mean snagging someone else's husband; I'm talking about situations in which you become the go-between

who has to do the communicating or reconciling between one of your children and your former husband.

For example, your "ex" says he's going to come by to take one of the children on an outing. He fails to show up and the child is devastated. It would be easy enough to vent your anger at your ex-husband, but it would be more productive for your son or daughter to get on the phone and talk with their father directly.

5. *Don't remarry too quickly.* I counsel women who have just gone through a divorce to wait at least four years before remarrying (in the hope that they will last for at least two).

Some single women might be thinking, *Easy for you to recommend the celibate life, Leman, but I'm the one who has to spend the lonely nights.* I'm not discounting the loneliness and the other struggles. But I recommend enduring a little loneliness instead of rebounding into another Swamp of stress by hooking up too quickly with another prince who turns into a frog—or worse.

You don't have to go into hiding or hibernation. When possible, associate with couples, if you can find friends who have a secure marriage and you are not perceived as some kind of threat. Being around married friends will provide a lot of security and good influences for you.

6. *Be choosy about finding a new mate.* A singles' bar is a possibility if you like meat markets, but I always recommend a good-sized church where there is a large singles' group or class. Yes, I realize phonies can turn up at church too, but your chances are still better of finding a prince who will not turn into a frog.

7. *Don't panic, especially if you have children who are depending on you.* As the flight attendant demonstrates before every airliner takes off, the adult should put on her oxygen mask first—then the child's. I think you see the point.

Samantha, age twenty-four, is a good illustration. She came to me for help when she was going through a divorce. Her husband had found another woman and left her with a nine-year-old and a six-year-old after nine years of marriage. It didn't take a calculator to determine that Samantha was pregnant when she married at age fifteen. She had learned the hard way, and now at age twenty-four she had the scars and wisdom of a forty-year-old.

During counseling she became concerned

—even tearful—because she felt her husband was going make a move to gain custody of her two daughters. I soon realized why she was so worried: She had dropped out of high school in her sophomore year and had no marketable job skills to speak of. To make matters worse, her parents were unable and unwilling to give her any support. On her own, there was no way she could make it with her two children.

Samantha was shocked when I suggested that she not fight her husband for custody. In fact, I encouraged her to talk with her attorney and see if she could get an agreement drawn up to allow the children to live with their father for a set period of time and then have the court review the situation to make a final determination. Samantha vowed she'd never allow her two little girls to go live with their father and "that woman."

"By your own admission, your husband loves the girls very much and is very attentive to them," I pointed out. "He makes good money as a concrete laborer and can support them. Best of all, he wants them around. They'll get good care."

"What am I supposed to do without my kids?" she almost shouted.

"You told me that more than anything in the world you want to help your daughters. If you mean that, you've got to get an education —you've got to get some training."

"But I have a job . . ." she protested.

"Samantha, as long as the children live with you, you'll spend the few dollars you make waitressing and you'll always be on the brink of food stamps. You'll never get ahead. Let the girls live with their dad for a while and explore getting some vocational training. Get your general education degree and then take a look at a community college."

With great reluctance (and some irritation toward me), Samantha gave in and allowed her husband temporary custody of the children. She went back to high school and finished up her G.E.D. in record time. Then she went on to the local community college to study nursing. She told me that as a child she often had played with dolls and fantasized about being a nurse. Well, she got to live out her fantasy and make reality work as well. Today she is a licensed practical nurse, working in a hospital for a fairly decent wage, and has both of her daughters living with her.

Samantha is one more example of how people need to use their heads as well as their hearts. You need to make a commitment to start attacking life. If you'll forgive the sports analogy, it's like playing a ground ball in baseball. The coach always tells his player, "Play the ball—don't let the ball play you. Pursue the ball, attack the ball, run toward the ball—*don't back up!*"

The same is true in life. Never back up. Never let your fears defeat you and fill you with stress.

Try the Scarlett O'Hara Approach to Pressure

Samantha is one of the lucky ones, but she made her own luck. Her determination and love for her children paid off. I maintain that if she had let her heart rule her head and refused to let her daughters go temporarily, she never would have gotten herself in a position where she could be a real help to her young family.

So often I see women who are stressed-out because they have panicked and lost control. Life controls them. While researching this book, I wrote to Rita Davenport, who has interviewed me several times on her TV talk show, which originates in Phoenix, Arizona. I knew Rita did seminars to help women learn how to manage stress and "stay in control," and I asked her to lend some of her insight. She was gracious enough to write back and share several of her favorite tips. All of these are useful for any working woman, but I include them here as a little something extra for single working moms, who need all the help —and hope—they can get.

Rita joins me in emphasizing the setting of priorities. She says, "For me, it is God first, family second (with husband ahead of the children), career third, and so forth."

She also is big on learning the power of saying, "No!" She observes, "You'll never catch a rabbit if you're chasing ten of them!"

I was surprised to learn that Rita is also a walker and she comments, "It's the best exercise I can think of to get rid of stress."

Some other Davenport approaches to controlling and preventing stress that I especially liked were these:

1. When under pressure, ask yourself, "Is this situation the worst thing that could happen to me?"

For example, you are running late for an appointment, you're bumper-to-bumper in traffic, and the light seems permanently stuck on red. That recently happened to me, and I simply asked myself, "Is this as bad as what happened to my friend, whose thirty-two-year-old husband walked out the door for work one morning and dropped dead before he reached his car?" Realizing that whatever is happening usually could be much worse, helps relieve a lot of stress.

2. Release tension by using the "gross physical impact technique" that features punching the beds as you make them. The more kids you have, the more stress you have, but at the same time, you also have more beds to make and punch!

3. Use the Scarlett O'Hara technique for handling pressure. Scarlett was always saying, "I'll think about that tomorrow." And she was right. In seminars I talk about how they train fighter pilots. The instructor tells the recruits that they can think about going up in their planes, that

the plane could crash, that they
could be shot down, that their para-
chute could fail to open, and even if
it did open, they could get down to
the ground and still be shot. The
point is, why worry about any of
that? Don't worry about anything
until you face it. Most of what we
worry about doesn't happen anyway.

4. Eat the crust first. Get the unpleasant things over with and use the
more pleasant tasks to reward yourself and give yourself new energy
and motivation.

5. Learn to go into the "Alpha
state" the way Thomas Edison and
Albert Einstein did. Use a comfortable recliner or the couch and simply
lie back and totally relax. Take deep
breaths and don't cross your hands or
your feet—just go limp. Close your
eyes and picture a beautiful setting
where you've been before and felt
peace and harmony. Maybe you can
even hear the sounds of the ocean
waves or the wind blowing in the
trees. Just drift off, but don't worry
about going to sleep. In fact, it's bet-

ter if you don't go completely under. Five or ten minutes of being in the Alpha state gives me rest equivalent to two hours' sleep.

6. Adopt the motto "If money will fix it, then it's not really a problem." For example, the air-conditioning compressor went out on my car. I had the $396 it took to fix it, but even if I hadn't had the money right then, the point is, *the compressor was fixable.* Once I shared this tip in a seminar with the woman sitting next to me, and she had tears in her eyes. She said, "Rita, I've been bitter about something for seven years and now I'm going home to fix it. I'm not going to be bitter about it again."

Money won't fix everything, but the point is, don't let the things that money can fix cause you worry, tension, and stress. I've had my house burn down—I know what it's like to come home and have nothing but the clothes on my back, but money fixed the problem eventually.

What about the things that money can't fix? I know about those, too. My brother has cancer of the lymph nodes. But I don't look on my brother as sick. I see him as sound, healthy, a good father, a good husband, and a good policeman. I am convinced that our minds and thoughts are extremely powerful. What we dwell on we bring to pass. Job said, "What I feared has come upon me; what I dreaded has happened to me. I have no peace, no quietness; I have no rest, but only turmoil."[2]

We always have a choice between the positive thought and the negative one. Why choose thoughts that will just bring more stress?

Rita's words are full of wisdom for anyone, married or single, working or "stay at home." There are all kinds of jokes about the "light at the end of the tunnel." But I really believe the light is down there—way down there at the end. Maybe you can't quite see it yet, but it's there, and if you keep looking you'll find it.

The seemingly unworkable situations will not last forever. Moments of crisis do pass.

Stress may get you down temporarily, but you never have to let it count you out. I have my own story about that, and I will share it with you in the next chapter.

11

The Night I Fell Off the Balance Beam of Life

"As I came to on the floor, I heard Sande saying, 'The ambulance is on the way. . . .' "

Ever since chapter 1, I've been promising my personal story (actually it's a confession) of experiencing stress. I believe the old line goes, "Physician, heal thyself." In my case, I had to learn its meaning the hard way.

Let's go back to Friday, March 29, 1985—a hectic day that ended a hectic week. On Monday and Tuesday I was out of town to speak at a convention. When I returned I maintained a jam-packed office schedule right up to late afternoon on Friday. Then Sande, the kids, and I all piled into our family van to drive 125 miles to Phoenix to attend a concert together. We arrived just in time to gulp down some hot dogs and potato chips and slip into our seats at the concert.

Sande and I were huffing and puffing, but we were happy to provide our kids with the opportunity to hear this particular group. At the same time we had provided ourselves with the opportunity to monitor what they were listening to and, as groups go, this one was quite wholesome—though noisy. The Boston Pops they were not, but somehow we made it through to the end. At least the kids had a great time. They assured me the performers had been singing about heaven. Quite frankly, it sounded more like the other place.

We finally got back to our room at the Holiday Inn just before midnight. I let Sande wrestle with getting the kids to bed, which was no small task because they were excited and wide-awake. I excused myself from helping on the grounds that I had had an incredible week and was totally exhausted. I was in dreamland in minutes, but never did I dream of what would happen just a few hours later.

Around 3:30 A.M. I woke up feeling sick and

nauseated. I reached for Sande to try to wake her, and the next thing I knew I came to on the floor hearing her saying, "The ambulance is on the way."

Sande was talking to the security director of the Holiday Inn where we were staying. The first thought that crossed my mind was, "The Holiday Inn guarantees no surprises . . . *this* is no surprises?"

I looked up into the face of a Phoenix fire department paramedic. He was busy shining a penlight into my eyes and checking my reflexes. His partner was trying to find my pulse and looked as if he wasn't having much luck.

Holly, Krissy, and Kevey were wide-awake and staring at me, wide-eyed and petrified. Sande was shaking like a leaf, and all I could do was wonder what in the world had happened.

It Seemed as If I Were in the Emergency Room Forever

They got me out of the motel and down to the hospital emergency room. I was free from pain but very weak and flushed and perspiring profusely. It seemed as if I were in the emergency room forever. It took about two and one-half hours to examine me. After giving me an EKG, the attending physician couldn't seem to pin down what was wrong with me. I had not had a heart attack, and as far as he was concerned I could be released.

"But what happened? I've had some kind of an attack or seizure," I protested.

The emergency room doctor gave me a choice: I could stay at the hospital and go through further tests in the cardiac care unit, or I could go home and see my own physician. He was sure I wasn't really at risk to travel back home.

I opted for going home. As dawn broke over Phoenix, our van headed south to Tucson with Sande at the wheel and the kids and me in the back. For once the children didn't get very noisy or restless. They sat staring out the window at the desert landscape, and occasionally shot furtive glances of concern my way.

I remember Holly, our oldest, saying, "I love you, Daddy. You'll be all right."

Krissy, our second born, who wears her emotions on her sleeve, just caressed me, her eyes full of tears.

Kevey, our baby of the family, didn't say

anything for quite a while. I guess his eight-year-old mind was trying to make sense of it all. Finally he said, "Hey, Dad, wanna play catch when we get home?" I told him thanks, but I would have to pass on that one.

"You Need a CAT Scan, Dr. Leman"

The minute we arrived in Tucson, I contacted Dr. Bob Johnson, our family physician. He was able to see me immediately. As Sande and I drove to his office, we tried to find a reason I would literally catapult out of bed in my sleep. Was it an upset stomach? a flu bug? some kind of nervous reaction that was a little bit serious but not really *too* serious?

Dr. Johnson burst our little self-made bubble of reassurance when he said, "Kevin, you don't wake up in the middle of the night and wind up on the floor twitching and shaking over nothing. I am ordering you a series of tests at the hospital, including a CAT scan and an EEG."

"An EEG is an electroencephalogram, isn't it? What exactly are you looking for?"

"Brain lesions—you know, tumors," he said rather matter-of-factly.

"Thanks," I said. "I guess I just had to ask."

Early the following Monday morning I reported to the hospital. In no time at all, I was wired up for the EEG, with electrodes attached everywhere on my head and IVs pumping colored fluid into my arms.

"Lie perfectly still," the nurse advised as she flipped the switch.

Hair by General Electric, I thought as lights flashed on and off and strange sounds buzzed in my ears.

Next came the CAT scan. As they slid my body into the long cylinderlike affair, I felt as if I were leaving on my own space odyssey. The whole thing gave me a rather eerie feeling. I suppose I could tell you I had a certain bit of anxiety. Actually, my feelings were closer to sheer terror. Would they find a brain tumor, or some other horrible problem?

But the CAT scan was negative. The doctor assured me there was nothing wrong with my brain. Some of my high school teachers would probably take issue with his report, but as far as the CAT scan machine was concerned, I passed with flying colors. As for the EEG, it revealed a ". . . left frontal-temporal mild slowing with normal well regulated background. The significance is unclear."

The Neurologist Nailed Me in My Tracks

Because I really didn't want the significance of anything concerning my brain to be
unclear, I was in total agreement when Dr.
Johnson recommended that I see a neurolo-
gist. A few days later I sat in Dr. Laguna's
office. During that first visit he did little more
than ask me a lot of questions. But he knew
what he was after and he nailed me as accurately and perceptively as Sande ever could—
and that's saying quite a bit.

"From what you've told me, Kevin, you're
definitely one of those Type A people."

I knew what he meant by Type A person—
the hard-driving, highly competitive, impatient workaholic. The nerve of him suggesting that I was Type A. Didn't he know
that I was Type B—the easygoing, carefree,
happy-go-lucky kind of guy who lets life slide
right off his back as he takes one thing at a
time?

"You've got to be kidding," I replied. "I'm
known as Laid-Back Leman. I'm the kind of
guy who, on a moment's notice, can go on TV
and make people chuckle as I give them in-
sights into how to deal with their families. I
give people advice on how *not* to be Type A.

Don't tell me I'm a Type A. I'm not a driver, I am Laid-Back Leman."

Dr. Laguna smiled and proceeded to compare my lifestyle with the actions of a Type A personality. The two meshed with alarming accuracy.

"You can entertain people and make them laugh, all right," he admitted, "but underneath that laid-back exterior is a perfectionist and hard-driving pusher. You're pushing yourself too far and you're headed for trouble."

I knew he had me. In fact, he had me nailed in my tracks. I felt as if he had opened up a little secret window and looked inside my head and heart. He seemed to know just how I thought and how I felt. When a man can describe me that perfectly, I listen.

"What you had, Kevin, was a stress attack," he explained. "You know, the body can take only so much. Our bodies have a way of saying, 'Enough is enough.' When we put them under too much stress and pressure, something has to give. The body comes to a screeching halt."

That day I began to alter my life-style. "Laid-back Leman" didn't make any speeches or vows. I just backed off and began to do things differently. I reduced the number of clients I saw every day by two, which gave me time for two rest periods, in addition to the hour-and-one-half lunch period I usually take. These two rest periods provided time for me to just get away from people and pressure and give myself a little space.

The results of my new schedule have been encouraging—and revealing. I am more tuned in and aware of when I eat too fast, walk too fast, and so forth. Now I am learning to mentally discipline myself to slow down when it's necessary.

I Had Been Hooked on Adrenaline

Since my stress attack, Dr. Archibald Hart, head of the School of Psychology at Fuller Theological Seminary, has published a helpful book entitled *Adrenalin and Stress.* He points out that we can become hooked on our own "adrenaline highs" which come from a schedule that is hectic, exciting and fun. That describes my old routine to the letter. When I worked myself up to that night of convulsions at the Holiday Inn, I hadn't been feeling frustrated and angry. I had enjoyed my usual week of traveling, talking to clients, and having fun with my family. Maybe the flying trip to Phoenix and the rock concert had been a little taxing, but it was still fun to be with Sande and the kids.

The point Dr. Hart makes, however, is that pleasurable things can stress you out just as effectively as unpleasant, painful experiences can. When your adrenaline starts pumping, your body can't tell the difference between a "good" and a "bad" experience. In fact, the "happy times" can be more dangerous, because you start depending on these pressures for a sense of fulfillment or "feeling good." This can happen to anyone, from an executive under pressure to an overscheduled psychologist to a busy mother who is trying to care for her family and keep several other balls in the air as well.

In previous chapters, we looked at a lot of stressed-out moms who were well into the Exhaustion stage of Hans Selye's General Adaptation Syndrome. Maybe you've been feeling left out because you don't exactly fit that description. Your life is full, you work or go to school, and run your cabbie service for the kids with no major problems. In fact, you find it all rather exciting. You get "high" by getting it all done each day. Oh, you feel tired now and then, sure, but so what? It makes you sleep better, right?

Beware. I took the same route to a stress attack, and you may be headed down a similar trail. Archibald Hart believes you can become addicted to your own adrenaline. I think he's right. He says:

> The idea of adrenalin addiction has important implications for how we respond to stress, because the very adrenalin that gives us the high is also the drug that causes us distress when used to excess. If we do not learn to "back off" from our adrenalin "highs," the very pleasure we derive from even healthy endeavors can be a slow form of self-destruction.[1]

I Took a Page From My Own Book of Advice

As I look back on that stress attack on March 1985, I see it as a blessing—a warning that I was, indeed, hooked on my own adrenaline and caught in a cycle of slow self-destruction. I learned to take a page from my own book of advice that I use on all my clients. One of my favorite bits of wisdom is that we should be accountable for our choices and decisions. Now I am much more aware of how accountable I am for the choices I make each day, which determine the amount of stress that comes my way.

It seems there is no way to avoid a certain amount of stress. In fact, it can be caused either by something unpleasant or by something that you enjoy.

As we saw in chapter 2, stress can come in the form of a pressure or tension you perceive as threatening. That pressure turns into a stressor and our adrenaline starts pumping. Result: You get stressed.

Or, as we see in this chapter, stress can come in the form of a pleasurable, exciting experience that gets your adrenaline pumping just as hard or harder than when you are threatened. The point is, stress will come your way. The only way to be stress-free is to be dead. One of the best ways to control stress and prevent it from exhausting and eventually killing you is to be aware of the need for balance.

Staying on the Balance Beam Is Worth it

I've always been amazed at the way world-class women gymnasts perform on the balance beam, that narrow little ledge about four inches wide, where getting a perfect 10 is no small feat. I like to compare life to the balance beam. Obviously, by now you know that I'm not very high on trying for a perfect 10. On the balance beam of life, some days we score 1.3 or less. That doesn't matter, as long as we stay aware of our need for balance.

If you look up the word *balance* in the dictionary, you'll find all kinds of definitions. For example, one dictionary will tell you balance is "a state of bodily equilibrium, a stable mental or psychological state, a harmonious arrangement of parts." And in this same dictionary, "striking a balance" is reaching a position between two extremes.[2]

I like that definition for "striking a balance" because it sums up what controlling and preventing stress is all about. When there is too much stress in your life, you are doing something to the extreme. It can be bad, threatening, or full of pressure. Or it might be something you think you like or even need— like a hectic schedule that is exciting and stimulating. Either way, you're out of balance, and you need to correct it.

We have looked at several ways to strike the right balance in combating stress. Our most important tool is our "priority slide rule" that we use when life's opportunities, temptations, and pressures pile up. But to use that priority slide rule to best advantage, we need one more thing: We need a game plan for life, and we'll look at that in the final chapter.

12

A Game Plan to Beat Stress

"Sometimes I have a good cry and a long prayer!"

While talking to wives and mothers, I often make it a point to ask how they keep their balance when stress closes in. Some candidly tell me it's hard to stay up there on the balance beam of life. As for how they handle stress when things get out of hand, they say?

"Not well at all!"

"I haven't yet!"

Other women use the constructive or active approach and attack the problem physically:

246

"Move faster!"

"I put our youngest in a backpack to keep him happy while I do household chores."

"Get out of the house to shop or whatever."

"Pray at 4:30 A.M. since child is up early. Exercise three times a week, take off once a week and spend time alone."

"I try to plan very full days so I don't have to think about what's bothering me."

One thirty-year-old mom with kids seven, nine, and twelve was a good example of trying just about everything. She told me, "I delegate some of the piles of housework and run away to the mall or the library. Sometimes I put on the headphones, pop in a favorite tape, and tune everyone out for thirty minutes. And then sometimes I have a good cry and a long prayer!"

We All Need Our Own Game Plan

This mother's honest admission is a good illustration of someone who is coping with stress the best she can by taking things on the run and doing whatever seems to work at the moment. Some of her tactics are good ones—especially the "good cry and a long prayer."

But what all of us need is our own game plan —a foundational approach to life to keep things in perspective.

When I talk to clients about a "game plan," I think of three basic areas. When life threatens to turn into a Swamp, it's best to realize you can control only so many things. You need to put everything in some kind of simple order. One exercise I find helpful for many clients is to take out a piece of paper and put down three headings: (1) Physical, (2) Emotional, and (3) Spiritual.

What is important in each of these areas? What goals can you set to help yourself find a way out of the Swamp?

Physical Goals Don't Include "Working Harder"

When I talk about "physical goals," some women think I want them to get organized and get things done faster. That approach usually causes *more* stress, not less. When I talk about preventing stress physically, I mean activities you can do that will give you relaxation or feelings of accomplishment and fulfillment that you don't get from the daily grind. In short, you should find ways to take better care of your body.

For example, under physical goals you may want to think about your weight (then again, maybe you would rather not). Because *dieting* is a dirty word that just causes more stress for many people, I prefer the term *eating sensibly* and right along with eating sensibly I advocate some form of exercise.

Perhaps you, like Teri, need to do one thing a week just for yourself. In her case it was joining an aerobics class, which nicely took care of an important physical goal for her. If that seems like a bit more than you can handle, why not just go for a walk—literally. Get up early, put on a comfortable pair of walking or jogging shoes with good support for your feet, and take off around the block as fast as you can, swinging your arms as you go. Some people find it helpful to have a destination to walk to—a friend's house, a newspaper stand, or a coffee shop.

If you're in good health, start with walking a couple of miles a day. Personally, I have found that four miles—two miles down to Dunkin' Donuts to pick up a paper and get a cup of coffee, and two miles back—does it nicely for me. Remember that you must walk fast and swing your arms briskly. Your goal is to get your heart pumping at an aerobic pace —about 115-140 beats a minute for most adults. It is important to keep in mind that before beginning any type of exercise program, you should check with your doctor.

Why don't I jog or recommend jogging? I have no problems with jogging except one: Pounding the pavement can be hard on your knees and feet, especially. I've seen a lot of people start out with jogging, injure themselves, and then give up entirely on exercise. Far better that you start out with brisk walking. Then, if you feel you are ready, try jogging. Another possibility is to mix jogging and walking in the same workout. Whatever works for you is what counts.

One reason I suggest walking in the early morning is that it gives you a chance to sort out the day and think through what you can realistically accomplish. Note I said *realistically.* As we have seen, nothing can stress you out faster than the "Super Mom to Do List." The perfectionist, gotta-get-it-all-done-today approach is a sure way to turn your life into a mess of stress.

Oh, yes, one other word is in order: SAFETY. Unfortunately, there are some weird folks running around loose these days, and they could turn your morning walk into a stressful experience, indeed. I urge my women clients to be careful about walking or jogging alone. It is better to go with a friend or take along the dog or your children (if they are old enough). I know some women who carry a cylinder of Mace, or at least a whistle. Most important is to not go through the wrong area at the wrong time. That's why early morning is fairly good. As a rule, fewer dangerous types are up and about—at least that's the case in Tucson. Your community may be different.

So, the key points to getting enough exercise are:

1. Wear comfortable shoes that give good support.
2. Use a safe, familiar route.
3. Try to put a little reward out there to go after, a little bit of gold at the end of the rainbow. I use a cup of coffee and a newspaper—you might do the same or think of other incentives. (When I suggest a cup of cof-

fee, I'm aware that too much caffeine can be a powerful stressing agent. Since my own stress attack, I keep coffee consumption at a maximum of three cups a day.)

4. Keep a brisk, aerobic pace. You won't get tired. Work into condition slowly and you'll find that your morning walk or jog gives you *more* energy for the day, not less.

5. As you walk, use the time to think and sort out your day. Go over your priorities and plan enough to do, but not too much.

6. If you're working on a weight problem, post in a conspicuous place the amount of exercise you are getting and your weight loss. A good spot for this kind of record would be the refrigerator door, or perhaps your desk at work. If you get serious enough, you may want to record the amount of calories you consume each day. The idea is to "declare yourself" to your family, friends, or co-workers. Then, during those times when the going gets tough, your pride will keep you going!

There are other physical goals you may want to set for yourself, of course. I emphasize exercise, however, because almost all stress experts recommend exercise as a great way to control stress. If you find it more relaxing or helpful to putter in the garden, redecorate the spare bedroom, or learn to grow bonsai plants, go for it. (For additional ideas on how to get enough recreation and relaxing activities to recharge your body's batteries, *see* the Appendix, "Your Life Should Hang on a Balance.")

Whatever you do, *be sure that the physical goals you set for yourself are reachable and nonstressful.* The whole idea is to work your way *out of* stress, not set up some kind of program that will give you *more* stress.

Emotional Goals Are Important Too

On the emotional side of life, your specific goals should fit your personality—how you perceive things. For example, you may decide you want to get more assertive to keep all those controllers in your life in line. Simple goals like saying, "Good morning" first to the neighbors, smiling more, touching loved ones to show you care—all these little gestures will build your self-image and confidence and make you feel less stressful.

"Showing others that you care" is Hans Selye's chief way to control and avoid stress. He called it "earning your neighbor's love," a philosophy of life that is a powerful way to ". . . maintain security and peace of mind."[1]

For twenty-one years I have watched my wife, Sande, earn the love of neighbors as well as complete strangers. I know a lot of people who don't like me, but I know of no one who dislikes Sande.

One brief example of Sande's caring lifestyle is the "story of the battery." She went out one day with $150 in cash to stock up on groceries. Later she told me she had to get more money to complete her shopping. I gulped and wondered why $150 hadn't been enough.

"Well," said Sande, with a smile that told me what was coming, "there was a woman at the gas station who had her battery stolen out of her car. The attendant was telling her a new one would cost her eighty-five dollars plus tax and she was crying because she didn't have enough money."

"And so you . . ."

"Yep, I slipped the eighty-five bucks to the attendant anonymously. What else could I do?"

I could have come up with several alternatives, but I know Sande. She is a pleaser who gets real pleasure—and much less stress—in caring for others. In fact, she is one of the least-stressed women I know. And she manages to keep her life balanced at the same time. While she is a pleaser, she is no doormat. She knows she has limits and doesn't try to be all things to all people, which is a real source of stress for many mothers.

In *The Stress Myth*, Richard Ecker lists a dozen rules he calls "Ecker's Laws." Rule number twelve is something every mother should memorize: "You don't need stress to care."[2] In other words, you can care for someone—your spouse or your child—without taking total responsibility for that person's happiness.

Mary Ann Was Married to an Alcoholic

Mary Ann, twenty-eight, married to Jerry and mother of three-year-old Billy, discovered her husband was an alcoholic. She reacted in typical fashion and started finding bottles of booze and pouring them down the sink. Or sometimes, she would just hide the stuff so Jerry couldn't find it. She nagged him, berated him, called his mother and had her do the same, left books and other materials around the house for him to read, all to no avail. By the time she came in for therapy, she had cared so much she was in severe stress. I told her, "You've got to let go of Jerry's alcoholism."

"What do you mean?" she said.

"You're not the alcoholic, he is," I responded. "You can't be accountable for his behavior. He has to become responsible and accountable for himself."

Mary Ann got the message. She stopped covering for Jerry with his family and she also stopped calling in to work to give excuses for him when he was hung over. She also refused to cancel her own plans to go to a friend's house because Jerry got drunk at the last minute. On one occasion she took little Billy and left home when Jerry came home rip-roaring drunk. He woke up at 10:00 A.M. the next morning and missed an important meeting at work.

Mary Ann also stopped holding dinner. It

was served hot at 6:00 P.M. and if Jerry wasn't there, he found his plate in the refrigerator when he got home, with clear instructions on how to warm it himself.

Possibly the key thing Mary Ann did was let Jerry know she wasn't going to "mother" him any longer. She told him in no uncertain terms, "I'm not going to continue living like this!"

Jerry changed in a relatively short time. In less than six weeks he was willing to go into an alcoholic treatment facility, where he really turned things around. Not only did it save his business but it saved his marriage as well.

Living with—and caring about—an alcoholic is a challenge you may not have to face, but how about your own family? All kinds of emotional goals are possible there. Is your spouse your Number One priority? He should be. Are your children Number Two, and does you job, your church work, your hobby come in third or lower?

Some devout women I counsel challenge me when I put church work down several pegs on the priority scale. Somehow they equate church work with a right relationship to God. My stock answer is, "I think church work is wonderful, as long as it doesn't come between you and God or you and your loved ones."

Obviously, emotional goals can be as varied as physical ones. The important rules to follow when setting emotional goals to get rid of stress include:

1. Choose something easy, something you perceive as friendly or at least not too threatening. Take the one-small-bite-at-a-time approach and trim your "to do" list down to your size, not someone else's. For example, saying "hi" first to Mrs. Jones across the fence is one thing; giving a twenty-minute talk at PTA is another.

2. Decide to see things differently and act accordingly. When you set an emotional goal, you are exercising your most important option: choosing how you wish to perceive life. As we saw in chapter 2, our perceptions are a part of us; they are a result of how we grew up. Perceptions don't change without conscious effort.

3. To care about others doesn't automatically mean you must be in a constant state of worry and anxiety. A verse in

the New Testament gives some of the soundest psychological advice I know: "Don't worry about anything; instead, pray about everything; tell God your needs and don't forget to thank him for his answers."[3]

There is a strong link between the emotional and spiritual sides of life; that's why you should include both elements in your goal setting.

The Best Way to a Better Self-Image

The third priority area in which you need to set some specific goals is spiritual. Some of my clients become a bit leery when I mention the spiritual side of life, because they think I'm going to "talk religion." I simply point out, however, that the spiritual dimension is a need in all of us, whatever we might think of "religion." Besides, taking a good look at your spiritual needs is an excellent way to work on gaining a better self-image.

Your self-image is not a fact—it is not down in black and white, set in concrete with steel reinforcing rods running through it. *Self-image is a matter of faith.* Tell me who or what you believe in and I can make a pretty good guess about your self-esteem.

One of the best illustrations of how faith affects self-image comes from the life of Paul the Apostle, a zealous Jew who was converted to Christianity while out looking for more Christians he could persecute. Paul knew all about stress. He also knew about battles against a poor self-image. In one of his letters he wrote: "I don't understand myself at all, for I really want to do what is right, but I can't. I do what I don't want to—what I hate."[4]

Paul realized his weaknesses and imperfections and turned to God for help. He admitted that he wasn't in the self-image-making business—God is. I often tell clients that same thing, because nothing is more stressful than thinking everything—including your own self-image—depends on you.

A simple spiritual goal to pursue could be just talking to God each day. Thank Him for creating you and loving you. Do this regularly, and your self-image has to improve.

Another spiritual goal could be seeking out a place to worship. Maybe you are like Teri and Joe were. You used to enjoy your place of worship, but you have drifted away because of one thing or another. Many of my clients talk about having "lost their spiritual moorings." For some, it's hard to get them back, but it can be done if you want to.

I realize that looking at the spiritual side of your life can be uncomfortable, even frightening. You may think that God has done you in, that He has dealt you a hand that is too hard to play out in this life.

Connie, age thirty-two and mother of three boys, nine, seven, and six, came to see me in that very frame of mind. Connie was a classic case of a princess who married a prince who turned into a frog and started jumping from one pad to another. In this case the other pad belonged to a woman he met in his job as a traveling sales representative.

After eleven years of marriage, Connie's husband left her for the other woman. Her story is one I hear frequently in my practice. She had been knocked flat by her husband's desertion. The irony of it all was that now she had to go back to work after working for so many years to finance her husband's master's degree in Marketing!

Connie felt trapped in her new responsibility as sole supporter of her children, physically and emotionally. After only a few sessions I learned that Connie longed for a peace within that went beyond the emotional. At our next session I did a bit of probing: "May I ask where you feel you are spiritually?"

"You mean religion?" she shot back grimly.

Connie's answer concerned me and also confirmed what I had feared. So often people tie the spiritual side of life into "religion." Connie was no exception, and made no bones about being turned off by religion. She had been reared in a strict "religious" home, but what had really impressed her was that all the church ever seemed to want out of her was money.

Understandably, Connie balked when I tried to point out that there were three sides to life: the physical, the emotional, and the spiritual. Every time I asked Connie about the spiritual side of things and her relationship to God, she came back to her experience with the church.

I worked very slowly and gently with Connie—sometimes it felt like walking on eggs. I pointed out that every human being can have a relationship with God and that she could rely on God for guidance, support, and encouragement in life. It took a while to help Connie sort out the difference between having a relationship to God and being a church member. But over a period of time she began to do some risk taking, spiritually. Interestingly enough, I have found that risk taking is one of the ways we all learn to handle stress. The key is to not take risks that are too big or overwhelming.

Connie began opening herself up to the love of God, and in time began to feel that there was a God after all, who did care and to whom she could go with her problems in life.

After almost a year in therapy, Connie began taking the greatest risk of all and began attending a local church that understood and accepted a single, divorced woman with three children. She became active in the singles' ministry in that church and began to feel loved for the first time in years.

It was fun to watch Connie grow spiritually and begin to trust God more and more. It was also satisfying to watch her stress level decrease and her self-image increase. I am convinced that one of the best ways to handle stress is to be in tune spiritually with your Maker, to have a relationship between yourself and God that you can count on. Belonging to a particular "brand" of church is not the answer. Religion is not the answer; God's love is. He is always available to us if we only submit our lives to Him for direction. He provides tremendous power through His Holy Spirit.

You Can Learn to Call the Audibles

As you work your game plan for preventing stress and keeping life under control, you will learn the important art of "calling audibles" when pressure and problems come your way. *Calling an audible* is a football term that can be very helpful to anyone interested in handling pressure. Let me give you a short course in football strategy that you can apply to your daily schedule (and also use to impress your husband some time when he is glued to the TV set watching his favorite teams).

First of all, you are your own quarterback in life. You call your own plays. In a football game, the quarterback gets in a huddle with the other ten players on his team and calls a play. Every play has a number and when he says, "28 H on two," everyone on the team understands what he is going to do as soon as the ball is snapped on the count of two.

But suppose the quarterback and his team

come up to the line of scrimmage and he sees the opposing team in a different kind of defense that is sure to totally stop play number 28 H. What can the quarterback do? There is no time to go back and get in the huddle again. Well, in today's terms he "calls an audible" by shouting some new numbers that everyone on his team can hear. The new numbers are signals to his teammates that tell them the play has been changed.

The opposing team doesn't understand what the numbers mean, but his team does. They hear the signals and know that the play to be run is no longer 28 H, which was a run around the right side of the field. Now they know the quarterback will throw a short pass to the left side, where the defensive team will not be strong and apt to ruin the play.

"Sounds interesting, Leman," you might be saying. "but I hate football and I don't care about learning terms like *audible.*"

Okay, I understand. The football season may be your most stressful time of year because your husband disappears for three or four months. Nonetheless, I hope you take the term *audible* and apply it to your own game plan of life. Whether you like it or not, you are your own quarterback and you do call your own plays all the time. Suppose you walk into a situation where you had one thing planned and find that everything is changed. If you go ahead as you planned, you will face frustration and maybe even disaster (they call that "being sacked" or "thrown for a loss," in football terms).

How should you react to the new pressure? How will you perceive the source of your problem—as a threatening stressor that automatically involves you in stress? Then you can do the usual: panic, get angry, insult someone, make a fool of yourself. Or you might freeze, clam up, and act as if you have lost all your marbles and the bag you carried them in.

When I surveyed different groups of women regarding stress, I got all kinds of answers when I asked, "How do you react when faced by a potentially stressful situation?" Various women told me:

"I try to joke my way out of it."

"I procrastinate, feel like giving up."

"I get nervous—I talk more."

"I bite my fingernails, get quiet and short-tempered."

"Become resentful and hostile—can't accomplish anything."

"Don't think clearly, talk too much, worry."

"Avoidance—I try not to be present, but that's real hard when I'm captive in the car and my family is having a 'heavy discussion.' "

The answer that popped up more than any other in my surveys centered around getting angry and not being able to function well. It doesn't matter how you escape stress. Maybe you head for the fridge, or perhaps you start nipping at the cooking sherry. Maybe you turn up the music and scream in a towel. Possibly you resort to drugs, legal or otherwise. The point is, there is an alternative—*you can call an "audible" if you really want to.* You don't have to see things as you have always seen them. As you use your priority slide rule, you can control your life with positive choices.

When your three-year-old spills chocolate syrup all over the stove burners, you can perceive it as either his personal attack on your sanity or an unfortunate blunder by three-year-old fingers that don't always hold things too well. At this point, you child doesn't need a berating or a spanking—you need a rag!

When your husband acts indifferently toward the baked Alaska over which you have slaved for two hours, you can go into a deep-freeze or you can ask him about his day at the office, which just might have been a dilly.

Of course there are times when you will fail and stress will win another round, but that won't defeat you. Even realizing what happened and how you should have reacted (how you should have audibilized at your line of scrimmage, so to speak) is progress. At least you are beginning to be more sensitive to knowing when you are allowing other people to do a number on you and more important, when you are doing a number on yourself.

Life is full of potential enemies: tensions, pressures, and even pleasures that can become stressors. You don't need to add to that list by doing yourself in. You can control your life by being flexible and audibilizing your way to far more victories than defeats.

You don't have to go on at life's hectic pace, wading through the Swamp, saying, "There's nothing I can do. I'll just have to keep trying to make it somehow—I have a chronic case of bonkers."

You can choose your own pace. Time is one of the few things in life you can control—if you want to. You can carve out those niches in your schedule, "just for yourself," not because you are selfish but because you are wise.

You can always make time to refresh your spirit, mind, and body in order to be able to do your job as wife, mother, and career woman with a minimum of stress and a maximum of joy and satisfaction.

I know it can happen—I see it happen in the lives of the women I counsel each week. Even more important, I see those things happening in my own life, as I practice with new commitment what I have been preaching to my clients these many years.

In fact, this morning I wrote just one item on my "to do" list for today:

PRIORITIZE THOSE PRIORITIES!

Appendix

Your Life Should
Hang on a Balance

That is, there should be a balance of rest, work, and recreation. For many of the following ideas, I'm indebted to Jan Markell, author of *Overcoming Stress* (Wheaton: Victor Books, 1983). Her entire book is excellent, but see especially chapters 5 through 10, and 13.

   1. Get enough rest. Everyone talks about getting enough sleep, but rest includes more than just sleep. Rest can be something as simple as sitting back and thinking about a pleasant place or experience. Rest can be taking a walk or just calling a friend. The point is, your attitude must be one of contentment and quiet.

2. *Don't overwork in an attempt to improve your self-image.* Ask yourself, "Why am I doing this job or pursuing this particular career?" Get out your priority slide rule and be sure you haven't been sucked in by a materialistic, consumer-oriented society that places the highest premium on having money and "things." As the writer of Proverbs said, "Do not worry yourself to gain wealth" (*see* Proverbs 23:4).

Hard work won't hurt you until it causes too much stress that can be destructive. If you work hard, be sure that you play hard.

3. *Plan for your leisure time well in advance and protect it.* Don't let outside pressures and forces interfere. One obvious tip is to leave the phone off the hook, or at least don't succumb to telephone company TV ads that try to lure you into using the "call waiting" phone service. Their pitch warns, "You don't ever want to miss that call." My answer is, "Why not?"

4. *Try loafing now and then.* Just listen to the birds or the wind, or just gaze at the

clouds as you stretch on a lawn chair or swing in a hammock.

5. *Develop a hobby—something that is ongoing and which you can pick up and lay down at any time.* If you have a hobby that demands too much of your time and energy, it really isn't a hobby anymore. Get rid of it.

6. *If you prefer a sport rather than a hobby, find something you can participate in and practice it at least once a week.* Be sure, however, that you don't get so competitive or perfectionistic that your sport starts to cause you stress. It should be fun, not a grim challenge or routine.

7. *Become a member of a small group—* a circle of friends and acquaintances that gets together regularly for fellowship and recreation. If you are part of a church, a home Bible study is an excellent choice.

8. *Plan regular times away from home.* Leave the kids with a sitter and get away with your husband (or, if you are single, get away by yourself for even an afternoon, if possible). If you're a working mother, don't call your office to see how things are going when you're not there, and don't race home to return your phone calls.

9. *Don't let the clock be a tyrant that rules*

your life. Check your day for "time wasters," for example, talking on the phone too long, watching too much TV, or reading too many magazines. Allow more time than you think you will need for activities and appointments. Don't set your schedule so tightly that you can't handle the interruptions or inevitable delays that come now and then.

In addition to the above, here are several more ways to cope with stress:

. . . *Recognize what causes stress in your life.* When your body says you are pushing yourself too hard, back off. Learn to read the signs that tell you you're under too much stress: irritability, sleeplessness, feeling totally fatigued all the time.

. . . *Avoid packing your day or your week with several high-stress projects or events that come practically back to back.* Whenever possible, rearrange your schedule to give yourself "breaks in the action" and time to recuperate.

. . . *Learn to live with imperfection in yourself and other people.* The flaw-picking perfectionist programs herself for defeat and failure. Perfectionism often leads to procrastination—putting things off because we are afraid we can't do them well enough. This only increases pressure and stress. Keep telling yourself, "if nobody's perfect, that includes me!"

. . . *Do everything you can to build a strong support group of friends and family members.* If your husband doesn't give you much support, try finding other mothers who are in a boat similar to yours. One researcher surveyed one hundred mothers in twenty cities and asked them who they turned to in times of stress. Ninety-five percent of the replies said, "Mostly we take care of each other."

. . . *Don't hold pity parties for yourself.* Develop an attitude of gratitude for all the good things you have. As Rita Davenport says, at least you can be grateful that things aren't worse than they are!

. . . *Use laughter or tears to relieve stress.* If you aren't the expressive type, try keeping a journal or a diary. Pour out your feelings on paper.

. . . *Control the amount of bad news you take in each day.* Watch fewer TV newscasts, for example. Don't stick your head in the sand and ignore the world and its problems, but be aware that you can absorb only so much of the negative.

. . . *Avoid unhealthy and unnecessary confrontation.* For example, certain mothers love to compare their kids with other children to make points and build their egos. When with this kind of woman, avoid the subject of children, or if she can't stay off the subject, avoid her.

. . . *Take life one step at a time.* Don't start a second project until you've finished the first. The rule is *"A* before *B* before *C*. . . ."

. . . *Don't insist on always being right.* To give in and come to a compromise is a far less stressful way to live.

. . . *Be honest—with others and yourself.* To always have to worry about "covering up" is a source of tremendous stress.

. . . *Slow down!* Don't talk so fast, walk so fast, or eat so fast. This is one I had to learn. I keep asking myself, "What *is* your hurry?"

. . . *Make a practice of saying and doing nice things for your family or fellow workers.* Be generous with your hugs (in the proper way, of course) and with compliments.

. . . *Build stress relievers into your workday.* Take a walk at lunch hour. Do a few exercises instead of having that stress-producing cup of coffee. Try not to take work home and learn how to wind down before you enter the house after work. Control your job; don't let your job control you.

   . . . *Tap into your spiritual resource.* If possible, start your day with prayer and meditation. Don't try to make deals with God to get Him "to relieve stressful situations." Stresses may still come, but you can handle them with a power that is beyond your own.

Source Notes

Chapter 1
Why Is a Male Doctor Writing About
Women and Stress

1. *See* Carol Tannenhauser, "Motherhood Stress," *Woman's Day*, December 26, 1985, p. 54.

Chapter 2
Which Way Out of the Swamp of Life?

1. Hans Selye, *Stress Without Distress* (Philadelphia: J. B. Lippincott Company, 1974).

2. Hans Selye, *From Dream to Discovery* (New York: McGraw-Hill Book Company, 1964).
3. Hans Selye, *The Stress of Life* (New York: McGraw-Hill Book Company, 1956).
4. Richard E. Ecker, *Staying Well* (Downers Grove: Inter-Varsity Press, 1984).
5. Richard E. Ecker, *The Stress Myth* (Downers Grove: Inter-Varsity Press, 1985).
6. *See* Hans Selye, *The Stress of Life* (New York: McGraw-Hill Book Company, Revised Edition, 1975), pp. 36-40.
7. Ecker, *The Stress Myth*, p. 10.
8. *See* Keith W. Sehnert, *Stress/Unstress* (Minneapolis: Augsburg Publishing House, 1981), pp. 28-30.
9. *See* Selye, *Stress Without Distress*, pp. 132-136.

Chapter 3
How Stress Prone Are You?

1. *See* Richard E. Ecker, *The Stress Myth* (Downers Grove: Inter-Varsity Press, 1985), pp. 29-37.

Chapter 7
Are You Raising Takers or Givers?

1. Carol Tannenhauser, "Motherhood Stress," *Woman's Day*, December 26, 1985, p. 54.

2. *See* Paul Clancy, "Clock Ticking on Marriage and Family," *USA Today*, February 28-March 2, 1986, Friday, Saturday, Sunday, pp. 1a, 1b.

3. *See* Naomi Schalit, "Kids, Women Show Effects of Rat Race," *Arizona Daily Star*, May 9, 1986, p. 2A. Carl Thoresen is also known for working with San Francisco cardiologist Meyer Friedman to develop the "Type A" behavior syndrome that describes the highly driven, overworked personality that is prone to heart disease. (*See* Meyer Friedman and Ray H. Rosenman, *Type A Behavior and Your Heart* [New York: Alfred A. Knopf, Inc., 1974]). Thoresen's conclusions about the high degree of stress among women and children are based on data from the Framingham Heart Study, a twenty-four-year survey of 5209 men and women, as well as two studies by Thoresen and his colleagues of more than eight

hundred children in the San Francisco Bay Area. In addition, Thoresen has reviewed more than forty other published studies on children as part of his stress research.

4. David Elkind, *The Hurried Child* (Reading, Massachusetts: Addison-Wesley Publishing Company, 1981), p. xii.

5. For more on Reality Discipline, *see* Dr. Kevin Leman, *Making Children Mind Without Losing Yours* (Old Tappan, New Jersey: Fleming H. Revell Company, 1984).

Chapter 8
Help! I'm a Cabbie and My Minivan Isn't Even Yellow

1. Dr. Joseph Procaccini and Mark W. Kiefaber, *Parent Burnout* (New York: Doubleday & Company, Inc., 1983), p. 9.

2. Procaccini and Kiefaber, *Parent Burnout, see* especially chapter 6, "Parent Trap: Accelerating Burnout."

3. Hans Selye, *Stress Without Distress* (Philadelphia: J. B. Lippincott Company, 1974), p. 129.

Source Notes

Chapter 9
Why Stress Stalks the Working Woman

1. Arlene Fischer, "I Want to Stay Home—Where I Belong," *Redbook*, April 1986, p. 96.
2. *See* Kay Kuzma, *Prime-Time Parenting* (New York: Rawson, Wade Publishers, Inc., 1980), chapter 2, "Sharing the Child-Care Responsibility," pp. 31-59.
3. *See* Kuzma, *Prime-Time Parenting,* pp. 55, 56.

Chapter 10
Single Moms Carry a Double Load

1. "At-Home Moms Have Their Say," *Tucson Citizen*, February 6, 1986, p. 10a.
2. Job 3:25, 26 New International Version of the Holy Bible.

Chapter 11
The Night I Fell Off the Balance Beam of Life

1. Archibald Hart, "Addicted to Adrenalin," *Focus on the Family*, April 1986, p. 7.
2. William Morris, Editor, *The American*

Heritage Dictionary of the English Language (Boston: Houghton-Mifflin Company, 1969), pp. 100, 101.

Chapter 12
Game Plan to Beat Stress

1. *See* Hans Selye, *Stress Without Distress* (Philadelphia: J. B. Lippincott Company, 1974), p. 21.
2. Richard E. Ecker, *The Stress Myth* (Downers Grove: Inter-Varsity Press, 1985), *see* pp. 91-93.
3. Philippians 4:6 *The Living Bible.*
4. Romans 7:15 *The Living Bible.*

Other Publications by Dr. Kevin Leman

A Child's Ten Commandments to Parents
Parenthood Without Hassles—Well, Almost
Sex Begins in the Kitchen
Smart Girls Don't, and Guys Don't Either

Other Family and Child-Rearing Resources by Dr. Kevin Leman
  Video Series

Growing Up Whole in a Breaking Up World

Love 'Em and Keep 'Em: The Challenge of Raising Kids

Sex and the Christian Family

Video series available for rental/purchase from

Covenant Video
3200 W. Foster Avenue
Chicago, Illinois 60625
1-800-621-1290

Film Series

Growing Up Whole in a Breaking Down World

Film series distributed by

Gospel Films
Box 455
Muskegon, Michigan 49443
1-800-253-0413

Audio Series

Parenthood Without Hassles—Well, Almost

Success Motivation Institute, Inc.
Waco, Texas

Creating Intimacy in Marriage
Vision House
Ventura, California

Source Notes

*Growing Up Whole in a Breaking
    Down World*
Way to Grow Series
Word, Inc.
Waco, Texas

Language of Listening
Word, Inc.
Waco, Texas

For information regarding speaking en-
gagements or seminars, write:

Dr. Kevin Leman
1325 N. Wilmot
Suite 320
Tucson, AZ 85712

DR. KEVIN LEMAN

You've seen him on "Oprah" and "Donahue." You've heard him on the radio. Now, share his good sense and practical advice in bestselling books that will help you understand yourself better and get more satisfaction out of life.

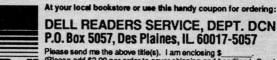